The Timely Lift-Off of the Famous Harlequin-Fish

The Timely Lift-Off
of the Famous Harlequin-Fish

Michael Glover

The Timely Lift-Off
of the Famous Harlequin-Fish

Copyright © Michael Glover 2022

The moral rights of the author have been asserted.

Cover © 1889 books
Ceramic fish, and photograph thereof by Joseph Dupré

Acknowledgements:
'The Report' and 'Strike up, Ye Minstrels'
were first published in *The Tablet*

www.1889books

ISBN: 978-1-915045-04-1

Other publications by Michael Glover

Poetry:

Measured Lives (1994)
Impossible Horizons (1995)
A Small Modicum of Folly (1997)
The Bead-Eyed Man (1999)
Amidst All This Debris (2001)
For the Sheer Hell of Living (2008)
Only So Much (2011)
Hypothetical May Morning (2018)
Messages to Federico (2018)
What You Do With Days (2019)
One Season in Hell (2020)

Others:

Headlong into Pennilessness (2011)
Great Works: Encounters with Art (2016)
Playing Out in the Wireless Days (2017)
111 Places in Sheffield You Should Not Miss (2017)
Late Days (2018)
Neo Rauch (2019)
The Book of Extremities (2019)
Thrust (2019)
John Ruskin: an idiosyncratic dictionary (2019)
Rose Wylie (2020)
The Trapper (2021)

As editor or contributor:

Memories of Duveen Brothers (1976)
Goin' down, down, down: Matthew Ronay (2006)
Between Eagles and Pioneers: Georg Baselitz (2011)
Robert Therrien (2016)
Monique Frydman (2017)

*For my dear Joseph,
who made me a gift of the
Famous Harlequin-Fish*

Contents

The Timely Lift-Off of the Famous Harlequin-Fish	1
At One with the World	2
The Land of So	3
The Light Footfalls of Thomas Gray (1716–1771)	5 – 52
Voicing	54
The Bird Call	55
Runes in a Puddle	56
Amelia and the Stone	57
Waving Back	65
The General	66
The Underling	67
The Little That May Have Happened	68
In the Event	69
The Report	70
Day Spring	71
Light Chinking	72
Yes and No	73
Leaving Again	74
Forgive Me	75
The Reject	76
Too Soon	77
I Trust You	78
The Easy Squandering of the Gift of Life	79
The Wind-Combed Grasses	80
Give Thanks For	81
The Heart's Knock	82
The Inscrutable Sleeper	83
Listen, Dear Doctor	84
Going Most Gently	85
Love's Disease	86
The Reckoning	87
Returning to the Beginning	88
Did You?	89
The Unsolved Mystery of the Pencil	90
A Tale of Discomfort	91

The Path Ahead Pauses	92
That Sometime November	93
the push and the pull of it all	95 – 115
Fully Grown	117
Fire-Fly	118
The Sea's Welcome	119
The Gottlieb Poems	121 – 178
The Death of a Mother	179 – 191
The Muffled Light	193 – 218
Coda - Strike up, Ye Minstrels	219

The Timely Lift-Off
of the Famous Harlequin-Fish

The fish, star-struck
and full-throatedly singing,
rose soaringly
to the challenge of its rising,

lifting high and free
of the ocean's chill bed,
feeling the water stream free
of its harlequined scales...

Did not the watchers beneath
look up then and marvel
at such droplets raining,

and such lashings of tail-fin steerage,
and such fish-litheness soaring,
and then join in the singing?

Chorus of Fish and Watchers

Such fish-flighty love
is all ours for the taking,
when we see her up there,
so star-struck,
and so endlessly soaring and singing!

At One with the World

Or not, as the case may be.
It is yours to determine.
The box sits between us,
the tongs, the matches, the scissors.
Make the first move.
I am necessarily a shy man,
with little to lose.

Take it up as you please.
Or drop it.
It is your prerogative.
When day surges in,
laughter streams after.
You know the routine.
You have counted the minutes.
Do not desist, I beg you.

The aftermath was as clear
as any throat cleared of its frog.
We two walked in step along the avenue.
There were pennants to cheer us,
a coffee or two in the cafes.
We were greeted by ones and twos.
We made a semblance of happiness.
The world was entirely with us.

The Land of So

for Joseph

He made himself just **so**,
quick, tidy, going at it all hours,
out of skin, bone and assorted matter,
trimmed, tailored, and thoroughly amenable.

So, they all said, **so**,
you've got something here.
Only **so** much, I replied.
So you'll be hearing from me.

There's a whole nation to be wakened,
sparked up, made to get-up-and-ready-to-go,
all hurrying towards the **Land of So**.
So what is to be done?

Now, I mean, or as **so**on as you say **so**?
Much, always much.
Well, I think **so** myself. Let's shake on it.
Less becomes more in a tricycle

world such as this one.
You order **so** much.
You hazard **so** much.
And in the beginning,

before the world's skin's peeled off,
you even get up and say **so**.
Did you say **so** just then?
Am I hearing you right, friend?

So I took the road
to the **Land of So**,
rising early, barely blinking awake
before I was off and gone,

so soon **so**aring,
and I saw you there too,
so gentle, **so** amiable,
and **so so**on to leave me,

such a sweet tongued **so**rority all of you,
so sociable in your **so**ng,
so soft, **so** inducing of **so**mnolence,
so soulful and **so**rrowful. Gone.

Here I am then, evidently **so**lo,
so low and **so**on solo,
being myself the **so**urce
of all **so** soulful **so**ng,

sober, just **so**,
in the **Land of So**,
in the **Land of So**.
Oh, it must always be **So**.

Mustn't it?

The Light Footfalls of Thomas Gray (1716–1771)

author of 'Elegy Written in a Country Churchyard'

A Prefatory Note

The slender volume devoted to the poetical works of Thomas Gray in the Oxford Standard Authors series is shared with another poet called William Collins. The two of them wrote so relatively little! Gray's fame is due to the enduring popularity of one poem alone, his 'Elegy Written in a Country Churchyard', which was completed in 1750. I happened upon Gray again relatively recently, when I was reviewing a fine book by the poet Jean Sprackland about the haunting of graveyards. The book did not mention Gray at all, which puzzled me. He deserved at least an acknowledgment, I felt, and so I pulled him out of the bookcase, and then, a little later, re-read his entire poetical works, the labour of a single afternoon. Almost all Gray's poems are marred, elevated to preposterous heights, and made almost unreadable, by a species of Poetical Diction common to many eighteenth-century poets, very different from the spoken language of the common man that Wordsworth and Coleridge aspired to celebrate at the end of that century in their *Lyrical Ballads*.

Then I remembered that I also owned a volume of Gray's letters. I read those too. They delighted me. Puckish, witty, and mischievous, here was the man, sequestered for much of his adult life in rooms at Pembroke College, Cambridge, that I had wanted to find, fragilities, hypochondria and all. This man was writing of what he saw and felt and anguished over. It seemed somehow appropriate that Gray's thoughts and observations and feelings should be embodied in a cycle of short poems, which I then went on to write. These poems steal many of Gray's own words and phrases. If you read his letters, you will find them. I tell you that now so that you will not accuse me of concealment. Any honest thief must declare himself.

Thomas Gray in Buckinghamshire, 1754

I shall stop when I stop.
Why demand more of myself?
Little is to be done hereabouts.
Much is to be *improved* by his Lordship.

Of nightingales there are precious few.
The Avon turns prettily at the foot of the Rock.
My friend will be abed until midday.
I sit here prettily. I sip at my coffee.

What more is there to be said?
None of us is quite young.
I have my rumbling ambitions, still.
Let me come when you bid me.

Old Court, Pembroke, Cambridge

Nothing happens at a goodly speed.
In fact, little happens at all.
I say this for the sake of the flies
whose habits I have been observing on this wall.

You may risk a word or two before Michaelmas.
What else must fill your days?
Cambridge sags in its fog of tedium.
I count the slow-spun days, miserably.

Two or three *themes* are hovering.
I may catch at them one day.
Pindaricks can be tedious.
A full-blown tragedy would be quite beyond the pale.

Gout and its Aftermath

My gout is gone, but I am not absolutely well.
Much continues as it always has.
I wander from my rooms to sniff the air.
When a spasm of piety seizes, I mutter a prayer.

You will tell from this how *level* all things are.
I would not wish for more. Excitations are a bother.
When a friend leaves, I wish him well
as I watch him dwindle beyond the meadow.

My life is clock-like in its regularity.
And this is how I would wish it to be.
I leave it to you to wish me well.
I send mine you-ward, whistling a pale tune.

The Ease of War

In war it is all too easy,
I say, having read the *Gazette* daily.
What falls out is inevitable:
when the Prussians roar, the French falter.

I speak of all this in my rooms in Cambridge,
The leaves are slow to fall beyond this window.
I slide the dust from side to side with my finger.
Contentment today is an unknown factor

for a poet, thin, small, with fitful ambitions.
Occasions that seize hold are few and paltry.
Caractacus was one, Odin such another.
Ah, to stride in step with a Norse god's anger!

Ducks and Doctors

Doctors please me as little as flies do.
They are also necessary.
News good and bad assails me daily.
I maintain this habit of walking, easefully.

Of Mason I have heard nothing
except that he has gone to Aston
and disappeared there, *sans plume, san mots*.
I feel for him as little as I feel for this breeze.

Walking, yes, can be a pleasure.
When a duck crosses one's path at the river,
its sideways walk, its startle, its flurry,
make one entire day complete and lovely.

Lady Cobham and the Ink-Fish

Lady Cobham has been dying at Stoke,
where I shall go on Monday
for a time yet to be determined.
Death is not to be hurried.

The weather squalls and runs and scatters.
After eight hours rain, a night moonshiny,
on the spin like a copper disc
whither exhilaration transports me...

In the daylight hours, I live deep in the Museum
writing volumes of antiquity:
Bonner has accused Sir Thomas Wyatt of high treason,
Richard III calls upon Elizabeth to leave Sanctuary...

That fish you mention is the *Ink-fish*,
loligo to the Romans....

Wild Scotchmen, with Turbot

Dear Mason, the world is as slow as it is.
New things do not reach to Aston.
You are in retreat from the world.
I, on the other hand, am abed, a little sorry

for the loss of our doctor, dead of a looseness
from a turbot, taken entire, on Trinity Sunday,
preceded by five large mackerel, full of roe.
This is all I can give. The rest will follow.

These Scotch specimens are wild!
Such ghosts on the tempest riding!
Not a Scotchman was ever born to poetry.
Foul smells may yet rise from the flames.

Macpherson Combs the Highlands

Hume the historian thinks them true enough!
On the lips, he blubbers, of everyone living!
Passed down, he says, from father to son.
Lairds, Majors, Professors have all said as much:

Beloved epics, remote and known by heart,
rarest of words, muttered by smoky firelight,
bellowed out loud from cairns and bothies,
frangible founts of poetical beauty!

Guineas fresh poured from a green baize sack
will send Macpherson forth to comb the Highlands
where great Mastiffs are named not Pompey, Caesar
(and even Hector) but Fingal, Ossian and Oscar!

The Abiding Dullness of Cambridge

It is now deep into sombering October,
and the gout has not re-visited.
With your hair grown long as you say,
do not expect to be glad-handed by the county.

That Lady Cobham had left me nothing
is a mis-truth, let me tell you.
The 20£ she gave me for a ring
exceeded her generosity to several nieces.

Summer was spent on a small, charmed hill above Henley,
blighted only by women who wore down my spirits.
Cambridge proved to be a little better,
the familiar soothe of its abiding dullness.

Some News to Wharton

Mason, being wholly attentive to the Beaux Arts these days,
has cooked up (with One Other) a sort of secret —
'tis a view of Mt. Snowdon with a Bard and King Edward.
He calls it next year's Exhibition-Picture...

The Duke is well over his paralytick attack,
though his face still speaks of it, you will see.
No more riding for him. No more violent exercise.
The best he can hope is for Newmarket in his chaise...

Heberden, in his kindness, has been asking after you.
His dinners are good, as they always have been.
To Mrs Wharton send my best of compliments.
Tell her: I am little changed from her memory of me.

The King is Dead (October, 1760)

This letter comes sooner than you may have wished.
It is to acquaint you with the latest thing:
A king, dead, in his chamber on an October morning.
I have heard no idle talk of a national mourning.

No effect came of the bleeding –
there were scarcely more than a few droplets.
A noise *unaccountable* had been heard in his room.
Between seven and eight, he had taken his chocolate.

Little may come of the passing of the king.
Public measures will remain unaltered.
Did we love him for his foreign tongue?
(Of Pa's manuscripts, I rather long to see the *blue books*.)

Tincture of Cantharides

God knows who will go to Ireland!
For a mere money-bill to cause such a prodigious to-do!
Too much detail for me to grasp at.
I have not understood. I have not even attended.

A severe cold has kept me trapped for weeks
between the pages of the *Nouvelle Héloïse*
and its bald acres of insipidity – dull characters,
thirsting for some *dénouement* never appeased...

I shall be dead before I wake again...
(Would you desire my recipe for tincture of cantharides?
I must own that it is much up your street.
The rich epicure lives to entertain whom he pleases.)

The Blooming of Aristotle and Theophrastus

Wharton, have you forgotten me this January?
It is so easy for a friend to fade into insensibility.
I send you as prompt a Swedish and English calendar,
with the third column (*very imperfect indeed*) by me...

in the company of Berger, a disciple of Linnaeus,
and the wondrously ycleped Mr Stillingfleet
who writes of his botanising philosopher friend
wintering in a garret to support his dependant relations,

a fine, cheerful, upspringing model of all honesty
whose wish it is to send Persons qualified properly
                          to reside in Attica,
all the better to understand the natural history of a country
where Aristotle and Theophrastus bloomed and blossomed.

Natural Matters, Here and Elsewhere

Speak well of me where and when you can.
Spring will soon be coming on.
Mrs Wharton's butter is everywhere acclaimed.
And even Deborah has learned to spin.

To Kentish town I walked in Jan.
Such flourishings on the S. facing dry banks!
Chickweed, Dandelion, Shepherd's Purse,
every one at their cheerful beginnings.

My calendar tells me strawberries ripen
at Upsal in Sweden on 26 June –
ten days behind Cambridge, I note.
(Ash drops its leaves here 5 October.)

Let Me Tell You This...

Of Andalusia one cannot speak with transport.
It wants verdure, woods and hands to work it.
Valencia and Murcia are one continued garden –
cottages of reed, earth sprinkled by artificial rills.

Wortley, it is said, left above a Million,
of which 2000£ a-piece will go to Lady Bute's children
and to Lady Bute herself half of the remainder.
Ld Sandwich is given some old Montagu manuscripts.

I tell you these stories to divert myself and others,
seldom anything at all to the purpose,
nor relating to anybody lately spoken of.
I tell them, oh, to stop eyelids drooping...

Such Canary-Bird Singing!

Lord John speaks of his pleurisy
as if it were no greater an affliction
than a hole in one's stocking.
He got it by going with some ladies to Vauxhall.

I would have you come to town again soon
to hear a canary bird pipe its twenty tunes
in my favourite Pall Mall coffee-house.
Such a miracle bird must be worth a visit!

The lines I have written for Montagu's monument
are poor to the point of indifference.
I attach them so that you might dribble your eye
across, and pronounce them unexceptionable.

Of a Fallen Column at Agrigentum and much else

Mason's *insatiable repining mouth*
cannot be shut, try as one might,
the reason being his recent elevation
to Residentiary of York, worth near 200£ a year...

I am steadfast in my love of Fingal,
though many doubt its authenticity.
These are true inventions of antiquity,
unless they be inventions of the present moment.

Young Pitt is back from Spain, unharried.
One who had been atop Aetna told me
that a Moderate man might hide himself
in the fluting of a column at Agrigentum –
96 feet when standing.

To Please a Yawning Guest

Something of the Sciatica hangs about Brown,
for which reason you may not see him in Summer.
I flatter myself with the notion that I may be shown.
God alone knows how that will be.

I have not lessened my opinion of your book –
best thanks for the copy.
The engravings are better than one expected,
though not as good as one might have wished.

The Press is to blame for much of this.
There is nothing that must not be said.
I sit on my hands, being a man of patience.
I let out only so much as may please a yawning guest.

To Mason Again

Must you fold your hands across your fat belly
in the manner of a Japanese divinity
rapt solely in the contemplation of your guineas?
Did God not declare: let them multiply
        in their own vulgar way?

Delap is here, having brought his cub to Trinity.
Fat and well, bowels excepted,
he has picked up mightily since his recent misfortune.
Would it not be happiness to declare the same
        of one's own person?

Louth's grammar is clear, concise and elegant.
His solecisms are gathered in abundance
from the best of our writers.
Does Hurd write against Fingal
        at the instigation of the Devil?

To Wharton Again

Were I to come to your Carthage,
would you do your best to greet me?
Do I sound a little apprehensive?
Before I stir, you shall know my motions.

It has been an untoward suffocating season.
The gout has been slight, after near three years intermission.
Have Hornsby send Lozenges
          to that poor sick girl my relation
who suffers so from a cough and indigestions.

There is little else to tell you.
Few have escaped without illness.
Give my best services to Mrs Wharton.
I have been these two months past in London.

To Wharton, through Yorkshire

The Earl has a very good house in the Q. Anne style,
with many pictures not worth a farthing,
together with a castle as plaything
on the hill's crown as a point of view.

Then on to Sheffield, set amidst charming hills,
with Talbot monuments in the parish church chapel.
The Peak after was bleak, tedious and barren.
Chatsworth, with its hills, shuts out
          all remembrance of same.

Indoors, the apartments are stately –
marble doorcases well done by Old Cibber's Father,
plate glass windows in their gilded frames,
and Gibbons in wood – such flowers and dead-game!

To The Rev. James Brown

I was not born so far from the sun
not to count myself severally flattered
by the warmth and approbation of Count Algarotti,
such is his name and reputation.

These little Odes of mine
were created for the Intelligent alone,
and how few of these there are
amongst my own countrymen.

Before he leaves, tell him of
Ossian, the son of Fingal.
Let him not be ignorant of
the fruits of our Northern Imagination.

Six Lessons for the Pianoforte

My mass of Pergolesi is all divinity.
The *Petit Bon* sends his love to you.
The rest are all dead or married,
states of a fine and equal balance.

W., who dined the other day,
said he wished to live here in perpetuity,
but soon returned to his Gallery,
with its looking-glass and its Gothicisms.

I do little to 'deceive my solitary days' –
but for a small smattering of music.
Send for six lessons on the pianoforte!
(Not the Opera Bach, his brother Carlo.)

The Iliac Passion

No events grow here.
There is a nothingness to my history.
Former days live in our libraries.
The heartburn has just left me.

I write to you *in propria persona*,
not as in my poems,
where I stand to attention,
stiff and upright in full-dress uniform.

Mrs Bonfoy is dead,
she who taught me to pray,
suffering nigh on a week against
The Iliac Passion, in great torture.

The Gifting of a Lyricord

Ld Bute has procured Dr Long his private passion —
an hour long audience at Buckingham House
where he gifted the K. with a lyricord of his own making.
The Q. asked *how he liked Handel?*

My exact account of the Heat & Cold
in the spring has yielded up this:
On 18 Jan, the small birds were so tame
you might take them up in your hand.

In responding to the unexpected honour
of a letter from Count Algarotti,
I lamented the painting and sculpture of this country —
oh, that we could exchange our tongues with those of Italy!

To Wharton Again

My excuse for not writing is this:
a lowness of spirits, occasioned by
the complaint I have often mentioned,
robbing me of the power to do everything I ought...

I eat less. I drink no wine,
and I am now taking soap.
Has there been some amendment?
No, and yet again No.

Mason is still inclined towards marriage
to a lady not fine, and small of fortune.
It may be a tendency to be corrected
with the onset of some maturity.

The Hour Perilous

In that perilous hour you offered me your aid.
By God's mercy all is now abated.
The soap may not have helped at all.
Too much foaming may increase the inflammation.

Of a Fistula there was nothing,
merely piles to an extreme degree
which, after nine or ten strokes of the lancet
yielded to that, and the application of a caustic.

And now I sail in calmer waters.
Only the gout in one foot bothers me –
such a *minikin* of a pain
that within days it had altogether gone from me.

Advice to Walpole on the Gout

When the pain is quite gone,
there will remain a weakness in the joint.
Take so much of motion and exercise
as you can well endure. Be strong.

Keep the legs warmer at all times,
well or ill, in bed or up,
than you are accustomed to,
but always at the same temperature.

Leave off the glass of wine that is your habit,
instead mixing a little spirit, brandy
or whatever else is palatable
with your water.

My prescriptions are simple,
but they are those of a fellow-sufferer
of about your own age.
Avoid, above all things else, filthy French nostrums.

To Wharton

Did I tell you? Madame de la Perriere is come over
from the Hague to be ministress at London.
I sate with her one full morning before leaving...
A prodigious fine Catholick, and no fatter than she was,

she kept a cage of foreign birds at her elbow,
two dogs well cushioned in her lap,
A Cockatoo parading on her shoulder,
and a slight suspicion of rouge on both cheeks...

Tell me how it was with *your* winter.
Mr W's health is quite deplorable...
He has been so sunk lately, but is now risen again at Paris.
I wish Miss Wharton great progress in her Natural History!

To Wharton

Mason's new wife has a constant cough.
For all that, he is exalted in his happiness.
Not consumptive, he tells me, lungs unaffected.
Never had such a winter as the one just passed...

As to me, I am in a fair way to be well.
My gentle stupefaction of mind bears me onward gently,
neither quite happy nor quite miserable.
My health of body is middling to tolerable.

Are you buried under the snow
like the old Queen of Denmark was said to be?
Spring up soon to surprise me!
Let your voice ring from the battlements!

Lapland Weather

Is Lord L. as good as his letters are?
And have *you* had word of Wharton?
I have been at Margate, Bartholomew's Fair on sea!
Not greatly to be recommended.

For six weeks something has been growing in my throat.
The lassitude has been intolerable.
If Stonhewer is to take a wife,
let her not be a fine lady.

Mason's wife is dead, I must report.
The consumption embraced her.
The poor man is lost in town.
We have had here three weeks of Lapland weather.

Kentish Fruitfulness

Mason seems not at all impatient to be married.
He models antique vases in clay,
and consumes ecclesiastical History,
when I expect nothing less than Consummation.

Kent is all a garden, so gay, so fruitful,
and of a gleaming emerald verdure.
This world, I have discovered,
is inhabited by more than two-legged cattle.

If my Odes are not to be readily understood,
a note or two may be superadded,
though not in such a way as to obtrude.
Throw them with violence amongst the end matter.

A Public Unsmiling

Am I not often disconsolate and alone?
The sores of this world are coming thick upon me.
Books tire of me. I tire of them.
There is no other credible story.

The days swim by so slowly.
The same footfalls pass daily.
I look out onto a court
which narrows of an evening.

Few have read my words.
You may say you have heard of me.
The poem for which I am known
leave its public unsmiling.

Gray reports of his Triumph to Norton Nicholls

I am in the sweetest of humours.
His Majesty has been pleased to appoint me
Regius Professor of History
(and Languages) in this university.

I had not invited such an honour.
It was bestowed upon me.
The salary is £400 annually.
His Grace of Grafton wrote handsomely to tell me.

I kissed the King's hand at the levee.
He even spoke to me,
though I heard not a word of what he said,
so hot was the day, and so complete my embarrassment.

To Norton Nicholls again

I lived here before from choice.
I shall continue to do so from obligation.
Here is other Cambridge news for want of better:
Marriott raises subscriptions for a Musical Amphitheatre.

Ld. Richard Cavendish is come, a sensible boy,
though bashful in the extreme,
All things considered, it has been a tolerable visit.
He eats a buttock of beef at a meal.

I have sold my estate for a thousand guineas,
and am now a rich Fellow with two gowns
and everything else handsome about him.
There will be curtains in days, and a mattress to lie upon.

To Norton Nicholls Yet Again

You say you have a garden for a wonder,
which keeps you dirty and amused into the bargain.
I have no such thing, monster, my garden
being in the window, up three pairs of stairs to be toiling...

How charming to stride out into one's garden,
breathe the fine air, admire a leaden statue,
a rolling stone, and an arbor
before pray-being-seated-sir on a bench with a fountain!

Odicle has been rehearsed and rehearsed.
The boys have their scraps by heart.
Before it is born, I swear it will be torn
piece-meal in the *North-Briton*.

The Sadness of Shenstone

Should it rain the whole summer,
Skiddaw will be inaccessible to mortals...
Shenstone's letters have left me vexed and saddened,
his wish for fame and many other distinctions –

living against his will in retirement
in a place which his taste had adorned,
but which he only enjoyed
when people of note commended it.

He writes of nothing but this place
and of his writings, and of the two or three
neighbouring clergymen who write verses too,
and are seldom in each other's company.

To Nicholls

There will be room enough for you, Nicholls,
but how shall Mrs N. conduct her hoop-petticoat
up the dark windings of the *grand escalier*
which leads up to her chamber? Do tell me.

The cure for my feverish disorder
has been sage-tea, life's beverage,
a polydynamious plant, take my word for it,
though not according to Linnaeus.

The banks of the Wye are a succession of nameless wonders.
My companion's journal will fix their fading image.
As for me, I am subject to great dejections of spirit.
Bonstetten no longer tinkles on the pianoforte.

To Bonstetten, in your enduring absence

My spirits have never been lower than at present.
Would seeing Wales change me?
Weather this winter has been mild and open,
with snow that did not lie. Frogs abroad 1 March.

My life is a conversation with your shadow.
I see you stretched at length on the sofa.
Will you remain so long uncorrupted,
with a beauty so uniquely frangible?

Beyond the cursed sea I seem to watch you,
imbibing all the jargon of French Sophists,
the allurements of painted women,
the vulgar caresses of prostitute beauty.

Nicholls, a timely warning

Do not mistake a *Caratus* for an *Orchis*,
nor a *Lepisma* for an *Adenanthera*.
Mr Foljambe has returned from the E. Indies
with such a power of rarities...

a phalaena, with looking glasses in its wings,
a Queen of the White Ants with tumescing belly –
such a jewel of a pismire! –
not to speak of his Flying Hobgoblin...

I have had an infinite letter from Bonstetten.
He goes to Rocheguion on the Loire in October
with the Dutchess d'Enville. In several provinces
the people starve to death on the highways...

To Walpole, in his agony

Man is a creature made to be jumbled.
Talk not of dying in round windows.
Your native indolence does not aid you.
Let there be no want of motion between the fits.

I write merely because you are ill,
and you have too much time to read me.
We live with a common enemy,
who now attacks us daily.

Why is it you are treated so severely?
My little expeditions are of some use to me.
They loosen me. They open me up.
Walpole, I know all this is scant comfort.

To Mason

Speak not so relishingly of your *old port*.
It is too soon to lay aside your horse.
There will be confinement, and much agony.
I speak as one who knows it, truly.

Confinement makes for this drift of days.
You wake again to the same read page.
You wonder a little at the odour.
It is you again, mirrored, baldly.

I speak as one who knows these things.
I speak as one who counts his days.
My friends, I greet them by their letters,
read and re-read, such patient lovers.

To Mason

I think Stonhewer not quite well.
Pray tell me how he goes.
Little Stonhewer comes a pensioner to John's.
He seems to have all his wits about him.

Foljambe, sometime a man of godliness,
has disappeared without trace.
Lord Richard Cavendish's residence
has been a wholesale digesting of learning and beef.

Wilson, we are inclined to agree,
is a good honest lad and a scholar
enough for your purpose, it seems.
This connection may make (or mar) his fortune.

To Nicholls

Do you alone have the privilege of being ill?
I have been one day only out of the walls of this college,
fleeing to the hills to take an airing,
which left me with cold and cough in plenty.

Capricious letters come to me from Berne,
the portrait too, done fresh at Paris,
no more like than *I to Hercules*.
Ah. to have met with Froissart means gifts in abundance!

Tell me, are you fixed in your house?
Or is Miss A. inclined to part with the estate?
That part blown down in the high wind –
how blessed you are to be so separate from the sea!

2 Feb 1771, Pemb. Coll., to Wharton

The old lodge is rid of its harpsichord,
its inhabitant lost like a mouse in old cheese...
Send Miss Wharton to a milder place,
where the sun will dispel all maladies...

Mason in town is taking his swing.
I have had neither health nor spirits all winter.
I must set down when swallows were first seen.
My cough has been three months upon me.

Bonstetten writes such vagaries...
le plus malheureux des hommes I call him –
much unease and confusion of mind.
Next winter he will pass in England.

Fragment

Travel I must, or cease to exist.
Until this year I hardly knew low-spirits.
Now an east-wind makes me tremble....

Thomas Gray died at Cambridge on 30 July, 1771

Voicing

I am to be led back to the beginning.
This is no shock to me. It is how it has always been.
Certain words offer themselves, nothing special.
I pick about, as if amongst gravel, seeking a jewel...

Nothing comes. Nothing sings out.
Let me then resort to the humdrum crowd,
amongst which I have lived time out of mind,
outside any realm of perpetual surprise.

Now talk as you might to someone in particular,
an old friend, accustomed to your voice,
            to whom it is familiar.
Words will thread themselves into a pattern
pleasing enough perhaps for the duration...

The Bird Call

Was there nothing but hatred once?
I remember no such thing.
I see pin-pricks of light in the sky, floating,
and a glut of heavenly harmonies.

Did nothing but evil stalk abroad?
You have surely missed something.
There was much quiet talk in corners,
the passing of gifts from hand to hand.

Did they not kill you too? Answer me.
I have no such baleful memories.
When the sword's edge swung down cleanly,
a single bird's call distracted me.

Runes in a Puddle

Colours never so brightly shown
as the day you showed them.
Were you there, once, to come again?
Frankly, it has not happened.

Colours never so brightly shown
as in that dress you wore, flounced in,
with that step you did, twice, once,
never to be forgotten.

I waited. I still wait for you.
Time hangs off the shoulders,
gives a man a stooping look,
seeking runes in a puddle.

Amelia and the Stone

Amelia

Should we call all this a refinement
upon the theme of you? Yes, let's.

You were never quite what I took you for.
Have I already told you that?

Forgive me then if I have not.
As I forgive you for being here, unannounced.

Yes, it was a shock, your arrival.
And now you must listen
because I will not stop,

having just begun.
It took a lot
for me to decide to begin.

(Looks at her watch.
Shakes her head dolefully and sighs, deeply).

The buses have all stopped running by now,
so there would be no turning back,
even were you to wish to leave, which,
clearly, you do not,

because you have only just come here,
and your coming means a lot –
to you, not to me, of course,
because I had forgotten you.

You thoroughly deserve
that I should have forgotten you,
let me emphasise that fact.
I had no truck with you for so long.

I erased you from my memory.
And now you are trying to pretend
that I was wrong by presenting yourself to me
in a slightly different way – more solid, of course.
Better presented, of course.
And not as a man at all.

That is what troubles me.
The rest I can put aside
because they are matters of
no consequence to me.
It is the fact that you have
rolled here as a **stone**
that troubles me.

You had better, I suppose,
explain why that should be
before you leave –
even though I have no particular
wish to hear you
because you are a matter of indifference to me,
as I have already made clear.

Stone

It was a yearning to transform myself
into a thing which would survive beyond rejection
which caused me to become what I have become.

It was not an easy decision.
Life was not entirely unbearable after you.
One does establish certain routines.

A daily glance in the direction of the sky, for example.
A circling of the foot
through three hundred and sixty degrees.

That sort of thing.

Amelia

The whole way then. The foot, I mean.

Stone

The whole way.
And much else, of course,
more tedious to relate
when one is in a hurry, as I am.

Amelia

A hurry? Why?

Stone

Because you would prefer that I be gone from you.
And so I must continue along because
your interrupting me merely prolongs
the agony of my life here with you.

Amelia

Life? Here? With me?

Stone

Temporally, at least.

Both

Temporarily at least.

Stone

And, yes, I do still call this intermission life.
I have my rights.
I own my precious vocabulary.

Amelia

Each to his own.
Are you then a stone
because you describe yourself as one

or because I perceive you
as being a stone?
Answer me that.

I do not understand why you were obliged
to resort to such extreme measures.
Your particular brand of mediocrity
is reproducible the world over
in so many more manageable ways
than the path that you appear to have chosen.

Are you then still a dolt?
Perhaps it was inevitable.

Stone

I am a stone for a variety of good reasons.
It gives me solidity, as you have already remarked.
It renders me invulnerable, to a degree.

Amelia

A greater stone than you
could pulverise you beyond memory
of your own final extinction –
which would, of course, be a great relief.

To me.

Stone

I have no memory –
which brings me to my third point,
that by choosing to be a stone,

I bear myself up and away
from this earthly domain
of near continuous pain.

Amelia

Why such pain?

Stone

Because you rejected me.

Amelia

Is that all?

Stone

It is quite sufficient.

Amelia

Any other reasons?
(She pares her nails).

Stone

A stone is a more playful creature than a man,
          I have discovered.
When the earth tilts on its axis,
as it is inclined to do from time to time,
stones tumble gleefully down valley and along,
just as fast as they are able.
I would be amongst their company.
I would wish to clasp to myself
such an extreme vision of carefreeness.

Amelia

At risk of needless repetition: you are a dolt.
Who cares about the rolling of a stone?
How interesting is such a phenomenon
in the scheme of things?

Stone

The point is this: I have elevated myself above
          the scheme of things.
The scheme of things no longer matters to me.
Nothing matters to me – to a degree.
Being a stone has seven quite particular virtues.

Amelia

List them them then for me.

Stone

1. It renders me well nigh invulnerable (I have noted your objection).
2. There is no pressing need to defecate or to eat.
3. The fact that I no longer possess a heart means that I cannot feel my own tragedy.
4. The fact that I have no eyes means that I could not see you, should you happen to arrive.
5. I am perfectly contented to live wherever I choose to be.
6. Time's urgencies have lost all meaning for me.
7. In short, I am foot-loose and fancy-free.

Amelia

Is that all?

Stone

I am coming to that.

Waving Back

Is this sand that still streams between the fingers?
Why did you leave it here?
By way, perhaps, of a perpetual reminder
of how you slipped through the cracks

with such speed
that no one had thought to miss you
until you crossed the border
and then so brazenly waved back?

The General

The smaller opportunities
offer the larger rewards,
generally speaking.

The general who told me so
laid a card or two down, quite fastidiously,
before raising his glass again,

and causing the emerald in his ring
to wink for the second time of asking.
We all agreed, unhastily.

There was such a studied slowness
throughout that long afternoon
of most gentle to-ing and fro-ing.

The Underling
for Peter

The two together, bonded in this image.
The light watery, garden indistinct,
pleasures uncertain, though she does look at him.
Who approaches? Why such gravity?

The photographer, kneeling, seems comical –
as photographers of that era tend to.
He is overdressed for a start, as if at a funeral.
He is pointing. He has started.

The watery light suggests thin rain.
Not a good outcome for such a day.
She holds herself tightly, as if shivering.
He is neither here nor there, the underling.

The Little That May Have Happened

Where you took me to.
What you said to me.
How you held my hand.
How you chastised me.

What the weather was like.
Whose guest appeared.
The nonchalance of it all.
Any daylight hour, any year.

What the words revealed.
Who interrupted them.
Truth. Lies. Infamy.
Street shouts. A scrummage.

In the Event

In the event of the deaths of thousands,
board up the windows,
stack the books against the door
to make entry well nigh impossible,
but above all cleave to your pledge:
I shall remain unbudgeable
when the winds blow inclement.

In the event of the deaths of thousands,
sing quietly to yourself in the midden
tunes long since thought lost,
carried on the breaths of the mothers,
how they brought honey down in golden pots,
and washed our mouths with spring water,
and gave you and gave you, and never stopped giving.

In the event of the deaths of thousands,
fling back the door before the final assault
so that you may give yourself
as a living sacrifice to one and all,
willingly, wholeheartedly.
Show them the points at which the nails must go in.
Pluck out your eyes and offer them now –
before the final surrender.

The Report

I am that I am, said God, in all honesty.
I looked at you.
You looked at me.
Where was the end and where the beginning?

So much to be seen through,
so much investigated.
A single walk in a park will not do.
Books will drive no conclusions.

And so we asked God about
our status, our natures,
our worldliness, our ethereality.

The report that He left us –
all those lessons in wonderment –
is in the re-drafting, perpetually,

by sun, moon, sky, stars.

Day Spring

Tamp down your anger.
Show a little patience.
New worlds are at the window.
The tree nods in the wind.

Calm all this restlessness.
Wash the filth from your mouth.
The future is eager,
the past soon forgotten.

Make walking look easy.
Do not bend. Do not stoop.
A greeting is possible.
Each day springs anew.

Light Chinking
i.m. John Ashbery (1927–2017)

Why have I told you this then?
We were together here, as one.
The balcony presented itself
as an opportunity,
together with glasses
and their light chinking.

It all seems too careless to tell you,
and yet I surely must.

Yes and No

When yes links hands with no,
it is then that the fears spread around,

merely an inkling at first,
a certain dampness at the seat of the chair,

a shudder at the curtain's edge,
the sky itself hanging a little lower

than would be customary
on a bland Tuesday in December

such as this one
is now condemned to be

forever more...

Leaving Again

I have returned home again,
to locked doors, low, grey skies,
and half-empty streets.

Why do they not speak to me?
Is there talk of betrayal in the air?
I catch a reek in dark corners.

Someone is telling me
to return whence I came
by the next high-speed train.

And here is your ticket.

Forgive Me

I should have warned you (forgive me)
that death steps up so unseemly quickly,
when a back is turned,
or the soup is not quite prepared.

It is then that you heel-swivel
and see that unwelcome presence
demanding to be heard,
saying: *no, no, it is too late to eat.*

Not here is the place now.
There is only elsewhere,
in that other country.

The Reject

From nothing then:
a wisp of straw
in the wind.

From nowhere then:
bamboozled on arrival,
wide-eyed, bawling.

*Thrown out, discarded, unremembered,
vilified, spat upon, shunned,
despised, rejected, ignored...*

The sum of it all:

a most unworthy thing
upon whom thy glory, Lord,
must forever be shining.

Too Soon

You arrived too soon.
We were not ready for you.

Some of us were mewling babes,
stupid in our infancies,
rolling around in cots,
swivel-eyed, drooling.

Others carried bellies
fat as balloons,
farting through the streets,
endlessly quaffing.

The rest went staggering
to their deaths,
teeth-rattlers all,
pitching forwards...

Could you not have waited
until another afternoon?

I Trust You

Yes, you were waiting in the end.
I saw you there.
I could never have mistaken you
for a mere friend –

even though your face
bore a passing resemblance
to him or her or them
on an everyday corner...

You took my hand
quite quickly, quite easily,
spiriting me away
with such a mixture

of gentleness and aplomb
that all I could whisper into your ear
just then was:
I trust you, I trust you...

The Easy Squandering of the Gift of Life

We threw away too many lives –
to the beggars, the undertakers, the anchorites,.
The beggars paid heed to nothing.
They swore at passers by.
They made light of these gifts of food.
They lacked passion for the soul.

The undertakers moved briskly through their lives,
apportioning one to a box, another to a casket,
quick-dealing in the truths of eternity,
fast-talking through tears, sorrow,
altogether crisply be-hatted.

The anchorites stamped on the ashes,
swallowed the flames as they rose,
muttered darkly in darkest corners,
stripped themselves bare
of all but our wonderment.

Yes, we threw away far, far too many lives.

The Wind-Combed Grasses

Did you say *thinking* just then?
You and all your tidy notions!
A bird clears a gate with aplomb.
You merely stand there, hesitating,

as if the world must always be too much.
You were always like that back then,
in those years before I knew you,
when you postured as rat, donkey, hen –

or so they have told me.
And it must be true
because the witnesses who spoke of you
were never

those long, long grasses, slow-combed by the wind.

Give Thanks For

The going out and the coming in.
The standing up and the sitting down.
The looking inward, and the nebbing through windows.
The bold speech and the prayerful mutterings.

The chance meeting and the planned convocation.
The easy walk and the dangerous uphill scrabble.
The less and the more of it, the true and the false.
The bright, clear skies, and the rain that drums.

The savoursomeness of meat, wafted through a doorway.
The sweet rising smell of the trampled grasses.
The least scurvy dog and the most handsome of brood hens.
The taking and the offering, the retreat
          and the bold passing through.

The mighty soar of a barn's wall, and the sputtering spigot.
The lovely woman who ranges abroad.
The man forever helpless, chasing his own tail.
Let us give thanks for all of this and more.

The Heart's Knock

Slept and slept until the storms passed away.
All streets swept clean of architectural clutter.
A long, level plain of nothing at all
stretching to the horizon.

Walked abroad alone – no one else to bother.
Lifted a head. Tweaked at a lip.
Nothing. No response. Silence overarching.
All songbirds vanished.

The light's lovely translucency.
Clarity beyond all clarity.
Strange shiftings of serenity within.
Heart's knock knock, as if wishing to come in.

The Inscrutable Sleeper

She slept for all manner of years.
Lost count of the heart's pulses.
Where was she diving? How deep?
Should I touch her?

Loved her for her pallor,
that quick shallowness of breath,
the way her eyelid twitched just the once.
For me? For me? No answer.

Circled her, round and about.
Pointed her out to others.
None but I thought her special.
To some, she was just a finger-post.

Listen, Dear Doctor
for Joseph

I want all this pain
to be over and done with for a change,
not to be scampering about the body
like a wild kid at play.

I want silence. I want the end of it,
for this body to be inert, still
and cold to the touch,
not all hot, feverish and rearing away

when they come with their bottles
and drips and their snippety scissors
and intricate sucking machines,

and endless pryings and delvings
and lookings. I want none of that any more.
I don't even want to hear of it.

My ears are blocked.

Going Most Gently
for Steve

A certain measure of inner disquiet
set him once more amongst strangers –
tongue-twisters, window-leerers,
blame-blabberers, throat-rattlers,
deep-delving insinuators, lift-crankers,
wild tree-swingers, surly bar-leaners,
double-bass pluckers, fiddle-screechers,
foot-draggers, brick-lobbers,
braying nay-sayers, costive spittle-gobbers,
and all plucked from the curmudgeonly sort
with multiple arms, legs, wings...

To go amongst them most gently
was his greatest wish,
to be borne forth across multiple heads
like the shrouded corpse of a hero –
all glass eyes, feathers and plastic nails –
at his own roaring and most majestic funeral...

Love's Disease

Could it have been you again
who forced me into position
across this table?
Why am I always so unable
to resist you,
with your palette knife
and your ungainly swingings?
Is it that I was born on this earth of ours
not to resist you?

Why do I notice you again
nestled inside my armpit?
Is it the stench of me that you admire so?
Or the enfolding darkness?
Were I able,
I would fling you forth,
snag you on all seven winds,
and have you borne aloft
until I am entirely, once and for all, rid of you.

Why do we love each other so?
What disease is this
which never stops creeping?
My eyes are wholly infected.
My thick tongue blabs of you
when midnight tolls.
My arms swings this banner with your name
through the streets, on and on.
Must I never stop all this foot-slogging?

The Reckoning

Make little of it.
There's nothing to be said.
His moments of triumph
are now dead,
as is he, sometime creator
of his own immortality.

Let him be borne away
in silence now,
as befits his shade,
king of the braggarts,
now pent
in the smallest of small graves.

Returning to the Beginning

A man approaches himself
at the edge of the wood,
makes a sign of greeting.
He chats with himself for a while.
He remarks on the weather.

The sky assumes smudgings of grey.
A small altercation ensues.
Anger boils over.
One limb is lost, two.
The mood of the day continues to worsen.

At the funeral, he greets himself solemnly.
Hand firm-clasps hand.
He hands himself flowers.
He regrets. He sympathises.
He wishes well. He leaves.

When he approaches the door with his key,
he sees himself at the door, with the key.
A small altercation ensues.
Anger boils over. One limb is lost, two.
The mood of the day continues to worsen.

Did You?

Much is makeshift here.
Much is of its moment only.
The hint of a scent on the breeze.
A scrap of paper on a table.

Much will be gone
by the next time you look:
the precarious happiness
of two roo-cooing doves;

that book you have been reading;
the brimming coffee cup.
Did you say goodbye
before you left us?

The Unsolved Mystery of the Pencil

At that moment of rest,
between one singing and the next,
he took up the pencil
and twirled it between his fingers.

When it rose as a helicopter lifts,
seemingly of its own deepest wish,
he watched it with a lightening of heart.

Snatched from the air in a trice,
it became once again
(as it had always been, of course)
the conductor's baton.

A Tale of Discomfort

It is not difficult
to prolong the suffering.
Even a small spanner will do.
The key is to take life calmly,
see it end to end,
be only as brave
as you need to be.

It is not difficult
to close off the light.
A twist of the wrist and it's done.
Let them all stand around
and wonder at the beauty
of all that is coming,
and how it might end,
never quite to be said.

It is not difficult
to choose enemies, friends.
One is much like another.
A winning smile may suffice
or a coin or two.
Shuffle the counters swiftly.
Be a little bedazzling.
Let them crouch, cower and wonder.

The Path Ahead Pauses

The path ahead
hurries in pursuit of itself.
Where next? Which turning?

It finds a river. Pauses.
On the other side, it quickens pace,
becomes mountain track, ever rising.

At the top, turns upon itself like a dog.
No reason to go anywhere.
No reason to roam, far or near.

It stares at the sky,
draws sky lines,
dreams of life as pure improvisation.

That Sometime November

This house that I chose is yours,
no matter how flimsy.
I live here.
You love me.
Remember?

Or was it some other
you welcomed indoors
that November?
Is it so difficult
to remember?

This your house is my house –
these pictures, these chairs.
We have sat in them.
We have stared at them.
What right have they now
to disown me?

the push and the pull of it all

The Death of Friendship

1.

There is condemnation
in your voice, your face, your gestures.
All looking is to be avoided.

We scurry past each other
like mice alarmed by footsteps,
your glance here, mine there,

with this wasteland between us
which once used to be
our old familiar spaces –

dirty coffee cups,
the slink of half-heard music,
and a drape or two idly thrown down
for conjuring a little night-hours' comfort.

2.

Did we condemn each other
for no particular reason?
The light in the garden is switched on.
You sit inside its pool, cross-legged, monkish.

What hour is this? I wonder
as I stare at you again,
stunned by all this old dreaming.

The nineteenth of December –
I remember it again –
so unseasonably warm and foolish.

3.

Am I both to see you
and not to see you?
Are those the terms
of our barren engagement?

I look at you
as you walk away from me,
needlessly hurrying.
The splay of your hips is so familiar,

as is the over-tight dress, always.
Why would you do that to yourself?
You had a perfectly good figure.
I say *had* for a reason.

4.

Who threw us together
that afternoon beside the river?
Was there no one else?
We had pooches then,
our common obsession.
All that picking up and depositing
in those black bins!
Such suspicion of our finger ends
when we held hands!

And then they died,
and we cried so in our bereavements.
Did those two dogs bring us together?
Or was it the martinis after?
I never remember swearing
to love you forever,
though there was much swearing
of a less gentle kind, old lover.

5.

I am as accustomed to the smell of you
as I am accustomed to the touch of you
and the feel of you.
You have always been
more than more than enough for me.

I am as accustomed to the flail of your arms in the air
as I am to the bustle of your body
when you rudely push past me.
Do you need to open tin cans
quite so speedily?

I am as little accustomed to
the absence of you from my life
as I am to death by drowning.
It is easier for me to believe in god
than to accept that you are gone from me.

6.

Let us try to begin a little conversation,
voices lowered, hands clasped, night-owl music.
You slide your glass towards me across the table.
I re-fill it.
We sigh together,
a single common sigh
beneath more than just a peek of moonlight.

Let us try to begin a little gentle conversation,
without too much hesitation,
without jaggedness,
without the spit and the spat
of old accusations.
I prop your photograph beside me on the bedside table.
I try the first few words on my tongue.
They seem to be coming so easy.

7.

You were a kind of gift to me,
unexpected, not so well wrapped,
even a little lumpish.
And yet I praised you for what you were.
I laid you down carefully.
I walked around you, curious, marvelling.
I prompted you to speak back to me by touching you.

And then you never stopped speaking.
Night and day you assailed me with your words,
so many of them so delicious,
just a few of them quite outrageous.

There was no picking and choosing between them.
You were who you were.
And now you are no more.

8.

A lover just now passed by the door.
It couldn't have been you, not any more.
When I get up, to look up and down the corridor,
I think I just catch you, looking back at me.

I can't hurry any more, not from this chair.
I am so tired of looking. I am so tired of caring.
You were never going to be what you were supposed to be.
This is the bitter pill I must swallow, daily.

9.

Word Rush

Do I mean what I say?
Words are so frivolous in their way.
We used to fling them about so gaily,
as if they meant everything and nothing every day,
every live-long, slap-happy, wayward day,

the same words, old words,
meaning not quite the same or always the same.
And then one day the words stopped coming
or they came undependably, slowly, slowly,
or with too much hesitation.

10.

The Puzzle of You

You were all guesswork in the early days.
I would tiptoe around you,
puzzling out the puzzle of you,
wondering how to twist you or turn you
so that one part of you would slide free
and show itself to me.

It never quite happened.
You lay there for me, bright-shining,
dazzling in all your intricacy,
seemingly beckoning,
cleverly beckoning,
and then, when I handled you,
saying: no, no, not that way.
To puzzle is also to tease.

11.

Once Given

There is no second opportunity.
It is given to us just this once.
Do I believe that now?
Did I believe it then?

The high float of your heel on the turn of the stair.
That look of you from the sofa.
How you slapped a cold sandwich down!
Such daily things, now forever lost to me.

12

Turning Back

Was this the measure of it all?
I asked myself that day,
pulling shut the door
on your sleeping body,
splayed across the bed,
awake all night,
tossing, bouncing, tumbling,
throwing out careless words,
half meant, half crazily improvised.

Was this the measure
of our love, our friendship, our lives,
that you should have said such things
so at odds with everything
we thought we knew of ourselves?

Were we that different?
Had we changed?
And might we change again?
I turned back.
I kicked open the door
to confront you,
blinking, uprearing,
dry mouth agape.

13.

Lippy

Those days are spoken for.
They have already happened.
They cannot be denied.
It is no use pretending.

We were there, both together,
loose-mouthed, shameless,
shouting them down.
We knew what it was to be right.
We had our old patch to defend.

We lived as we lived.
That was the nature of our game.
They had to accept it.
Our mouths were set in surly defiance.

14

Street Whisperings

Those street whisperings
are your words and mine,
blown outdoors,
floating now in the common air.
There is no wiping them out.
They are not going anywhere.

No matter how deeply we huddle here,
denying ourselves, the truth is

we were so good at public brawls,
bare-knuckled pugilism in the common cause,
street spectacles to amuse our friends,
bringing such dismay to
the flutter of the neighbours' curtains:
oh no, not those two again!

And now we are settled here,
over sighs and such
gentle, over-easy recriminations,
clutching the bottle,
crooning to each other
in voices as croaky-silky
as all imagined worlds to be future-conjured –
star-dust-blessed, cigar-fumy.

15.

Was that the last of our conversations?
How could it ever have occurred to me?
Had I known, I would have spared the anger,
the frustrations.
We would both have held off, surely,
on the mutual recriminations.

We would have loved each other more fully,
clasped hands, exchanged gifts,
spoken of all our old sweetnesses.
There might even have been
more ridiculous chat about nude bathing.

And yet we did not.
We were like cats.

We were the same old
fat cats to each other,
brutal, out-lashing.

16

Is all this less or more?
Or is it the same as before?
With the windows flung back,
morning blows in, chill, sobering.
We huddle into our coats.
We go to buy the milk.

The fetid air follows us out of doors
like street kids calling at our backs.
Ignore. Acknowledge. Confront. Kick ass –
you, mine; me, yours...

17.

There is chance.
There is also blundering,
silly flailings around, as if we'll
never get to the bottom of it.

Which is true, of course.
There is no truth.
There is no neat
ending to any of this.

There is merely the fact of our being here,
numbers one and two,

a couple of washed up, hosed down,
helpless lives, unlovely, inseparable.

18.

Your name was written on the air that balmy night,
when I first caught sight of you,
like a trick of cigarette smoke
blown through the lips,
intricate, fragile, delicately curvy,
and just as quickly gone again
when the air thought to make off with it...

I had kept it though –
a balled up piece of string in my pocket,
and I fingered it all night long as I spoke to you,
over drinks, at different tables...
Yes, it was not just your name
that was there that night.
It was you too, my love,
in all the fulness of your body.

19.

This much, surely, is given:

two hearts beating in unison,
fingers intermeshing,
two voices speaking
in orderly succession –

not random noises scrambled together,
with one voice trying to beat the other into submission,
not fingers scratching and tearing and clawing,
not two hearts shocked dead in misery and consternation...

20.

You have laid claim to so much –
truth, for example, good taste,
or those gilt-edged coffee cups...
Mumbling, I, sit here,
testing my own endurance,
occasionally smoking a cigarette or two
or quick-flickering the edges
of the pages of this book.

21.

If it happens to be true
that I more than care for you,
there will be consequences, surely,
for our future lives...

That is why I would ask you
not too leave too soon,
with your coat half on,
nor to leave your sandwich half-eaten,
and your coffee half-drunk.
Should we not just sit here, quietly, as one,
and carve out a little time for patience?

22.

This much and more
between here and the door.

A little steadiness
before the word heaven is spoken.

Caught on the hop.
Dropped carelessly, smashed.

Two large gifts in a very small box.
A parade ground for harshness and hostility.

23.

No one had asked for it again,
all the commotion.
It was all too soon.
The bruising was still so livid.
And yet the afternoon slid in
like a slow train approaching.

Sometimes I harbour
this wish to go under.
It would mean peace.
It would mean total surrender
to the end and beyond.

24.

That was surely the best
of our wasted days together,
where no one really cared,
and nothing seemed to matter,

and bodies slid past us,
popping like fat balloons,
and there was always so much laughter,
yes, always too much laughter.

And you said what you said,
and I believed not a word of it
because you were mouthing off,
and I would catch you at it.

You cried in the dark, and I cried with you,
for night and all its darkness,
for day, the glut of daylight.
There was nothing not to cry for.

25.

I sought you here and there
once you had left me.
There was always time –
more, and yet more to spare –
to be looking for you,
even when I could not dare to hope
that I would ever find you.

And I knew I had not found you,
even when I found you, here and there,
it was not truly you any more.
You had changed – as life does change –
into a different species of being,
more rock, more mineral, than human.

The nature of your voice had changed too –
fleeter, more flute-like, more distant –
and how you carried yourself on the wind,
surely too light for what you had always been.
Yes, it was you again,
some part of we two again
seemed to be claiming,

and yet, all the same,
it was not truly you.
You could never be the same,
not now that you had gone from me,
and I felt that like a nail driven into a wall,
that determinedly.

26.

Let's confess it then –
something to be agreed upon! –
we were an unholy mess
of human detritus,
as ignoble as it gets,
chaff on the wind.

Did you care at all?
Less and less.

And nor did I.
We did what we could
with our lives, all that trash,
pushed, from here to there,
yet never, not quite, going,
until, in the end,
it all faltered and stopped
like a junked clock
in an old cardboard box.

Here's to the past then,
and all there was of it!
May it forever shine down on us,
though tarnished (somewhat).

27.

Whose lives were we living,
so freely, so carelessly, so unstoppably?
Ours, or other people's?
No one – ourselves included – seemed to know.
That was the nature of our human community,
a blur of bodies with, occasionally,
some small antenna of a mind poking up
from the massed quivering heap
of all our passing, posing,
pissing and pissed on deliciousnesses.

28.

You wish for something.
You go on wishing.

There is time on your side.
Mornings. Noons. Evenings.

We make of it what we will.
We conjure a life together.
We hook up, clasp hands, smooch like dogs.
We are all there is to each other.

Nightfall. Clunk. Each one retreats into a separate corner,
examining wounds, reprising stuttered conversations.
Is this how life went in the end?
Wasn't, there, always, more of it, and just for the asking?

29.

You drove straight past me.
I didn't see you until you were gone from me.
In former times you would have raised a hand,
you would have waved at me.

Am I to complain about you,
to say what a bitch you were
to drive along like that
just as if it were any other day,

and I were no one, just a walker,
a street walker, making my way?
Should I complain about that?
Should I have jumped out in front of you

and screamed into your face
to make you see me again?
Such foolish, idle dreamscapes
of these lonely days.

30.

Wait and see,
I would have said,
had you asked me.
But you did not ask me.

You struck a match,
you took one puff,
you put it out,
and then you walked off,

proud to be hammering
those heels down so hard
in that street
that was racing ahead of you.

31.

Can there be more than this?
I keep on asking myself.
My head slow-tolls like a bell.
The sky looks grease-stained.

Mornings I get up, slowly.
That's more than enough.
The simplest way is a chair
to be looking out from

at nothing much better than this,
the slow drift of people out there,
how they make much of
a casual walk to the shops.

32.

In the time between
being here and arriving there,
you had changed your mind, it seems,
which is why you left me
to give an account of your absence,
improvising wildly, confused,
flustered, furious.

You said nothing later.
You merely lay in bed,
on your side, and fumed
when I accused you of
embarrassing me
to the nth degree.

The nth degree! you mocked.
Isn't that a mathematical turn of phrase?
Which is why, you must understand,
I threw something at you
quite as emphatic as a porcelain dog
which, of course, shattered.

33.

I said yes to you,
and that woke up, that single word,
the entirety of this world to me.
How could it have happened like that
when everything, always,
had been so humdrum, so humble, so makeshift?

34.

You have begun to wake me up,
the little that there is of me.
Very slowly I come to,
arriving here from the less and the more
of some far dream of me.

Yes, you say, yes, touching my lip.
Your idling presence looks so spectral,
looming in front of me
and then fading back.
I raise a hand in my turn to touch you.

I reach out for your name
from amongst every possibility.
There is no need to be quite so particular, you tell me.
I could be any one of those names.
In fact, I could be anything that you make of me.

Fully Grown
for David

To carry a child
in a father's arms
back from the seashore
is to bear a burden so precious
that tears are not the half of it.

So drop it then.
Set him down, running,
then walking, slower of pace,
carrying books, pencils, pens,
all the world's needfuls
for the fullness of
grown discontentment.

Fire-Fly

Yes, this must surely be the answer to
all our vague wishings,
those night-hours' whisperings,
to have you surely in front of me

as a rock stands proud on its eminence.
We take our bearings from it.
We even lean against it.
That will be you as I'll know you then –

steadfast, secure, ever with me,
but until such time as this happens,
you will be this wisp, this fire-fly here and gone,
this happening so tantalisingly fleeting.

The Sea's Welcome

No, not when you first saw me.
Later, much later.
By which time the tide was out,
and the sun had disappeared.

Yes, it was all strangely hushed
as you approached me,
and my back was turned, I remember,
so that when I saw you

the surprise was mutual –
because the sun had re-emerged,
the tide lapped at our toes,
and we entered the sea together.

The Gottlieb Poems

for Jason

Reading the Book of Gottlieb

When Gottlieb told his story,
the Pelican Armies faltered
on their long retreat from Moscow.

When Gottlieb told his story,
the Olympic sprinter froze in mid-stride
inches before the finishing line.

When Gottlieb told his story,
the suicide bombers gorged on tea and cake
with the Prophets of Destruction
just this side of the Gates of Paradise.

When Gottlieb told his story,
you – or you and you – of a sudden decided,
and it was all done and dusted
with a mighty resounding silence.

Gottlieb as Castle Perilous

Gottlieb has his dreams of the coming days,
and they are always sufficient unto his needs.

Several involve a bicycle or two
in which he sits propped high in the saddle,

surveying the wonder of all that is his –
the castellated walls, the sheepfolds,

the acres of wind-combed wheat.
What a marvel he is, this Gottlieb,

to have arrived in this place
without warning one day,

and then to be accepted with such ease
as if he were a scion of his own native ground,

and not a stranger at all
perilously protected by

his own bewilderments,
the very embodiment of Castle Perilous!

Gottlieb's Workaday Habits

Gottlieb grubs around for meaning
in the dirt at the roadside.

The growl of trucks passing by does not bother him.
When a cat shoulders him over,

he struggles to his feet again,
proud to fight back against

his own humiliations, albeit gently –
the cat passed by long ago.

How many lives has he lived?
How many gestures of majesty

has he flung to the four winds?
Many. Oh, many.

That is why he is so pleased with himself
when darkness falls with a tremor

and he wraps himself in a blanket –
as if he were this random gift

offered to precisely no one.

Gottlieb as a Grub

Gottlieb, are you this harmless grub
squeezed between thumb and finger,
so soft, so pliable?

Is this how you see yourself today
as you lean from the window
like an articulated table lamp,

and smile at all the passers by,
so pleased to be seen,
so pleased to be known

in all the nakedness
of your upper torso?

Gottlieb's Secret Cache

Gottlieb has been counting his good fortune.
The bricks which fell from the sky –
his future dwelling place.
The river that flowed past his door –
the means to slake his thirst.
The sheep that rubbed up against his thigh –
meat in plenty.

He has given thanks for all of this
by building a repository of dreams
in a small, proud leather box
contained within a soft pouch
lodged behind his extravagant dentures.

Gottlieb's Prayer of Mock-Innocence

Make of me what you will,
prayed Gottlieb,
seemingly peaceable.
Fashion me from bolts of silk,
random tassels,
dust-choked offcuts
of nameless fabrics
found, years before,
on a mouldering bed
behind the sanctuary.

I am biddable.

(This confession, it has to be said,
fails to take account of
the years he has spent creating
a ruthless armoury from:
keen-edged Hoplite spears,
Agincourt bows (short and long),
Tommy guns,
and a bevy of
nasty, Baltimore-fashioned
sideways slashers.)

According to Gottlieb

Gottlieb's life
has the keenest of keen edges,
seldom blunted.

Gottlieb's life
is a quantity
known only to himself.

Gottlieb's life
is small-screen entertainment,
with a bottle.

Gottlieb's life
is a sad affair,
often bungled, usually misplaced.

Gottlieb's life is defined by
an inward strut
and an outward limp.

Calling Gottlieb Home

Was that your whistle
I last heard on the patio,
calling the coyote home,
pleading again for heaven's gifts to fall?

It could have been you.
It could have been your likeness.

Were those your pleasantries I fenced with
as we ran amok
amongst the sand dunes,
spitting fury, spitting sea-spray?

It could have been you.
It could have been your likeness.

Were those your footprints I recognised
on the forest's floor,
keeping pace with the mother bear,
teaching the tender cubs your mysterious alphabet?

It could have been you.
It could have been your likeness.

Gottlieb's Tentative Removal

Gottlieb, my dear...
(I say it in such a whisper),
you were that gift left to me
one morning on the parlour floor.

So still you were
that when I came to edge at you
with my foot, you scarcely stirred.

I had to coax you down the back roads
to the ravine's edge –
that deathly yawning space.

How I wept to be rid of you!
How you return to me now, repeatedly!

The Sore Points of Gottlieb

Gottlieb, you slow-weeping sore,
is there nothing I can do to be cured of you?
Must you forever be here,
a stain on my reputation,
a disfigurement of my body?

When I set you apart from me,
I watched you walking away, haltingly,
on your dwindling legs.
The horizon line seemed to be beckoning.
You diminished to a pin-prick, albeit one
still furiously waving.

Now you have erupted again,
here and there, and always in the night hours.
I balance a cooling brick on a patch of skin,
another furious eruption I cover with my hand.
You are never not a part of me.

Gottlieb's Maddening Insistence

Gottlieb's moan is unlike any other.

It curves down through the air
like a slow-burning tragedy.

It is a ship's whistle,
drifting into harbour

or the sleeping cry of a widow
long decades after.

It is my childhood home again,
reduced to rubble.

It is that moment you turned away,
and I lost my footing.

Gottlieb, I say, Gottlieb,
can you never be silent?

Step Forth Then, Gottlieb!

I have the wit, the eye,
and the determination
of the practised maker.

I have the nuts, the screws,
the bolts, the planks,
and the necessary tools.

I have the will, the aplomb,
the plumb line and,
needless to say,
the idle hours stretching away.

I have the workshop
with its yawning spaces,
and the ferocity
of the light bulb, naked.

I have money in the bank,
strength in the arm,
a certain keenness of look,
and a ferocious appetite.

I have the urge to begin,
gain pace,
and push through
to the bitter-sweet end.

Step forth from the shadows then,
Gottlieb, coy child.
Do not pretend
to pretend.

Gottlieb Makes a Public Spectacle of Himself to General Derision

Gottlieb scrawls the word again,
over and over, with a stick,
in the drifting sand.
L.O.V.E. L.O.V.E.
L.O.V.E. L.O.V.E.

He never quite gets it right.
It is always a jumble of letters
in no particular order.
He weeps with frustration.
He tears at his own body.

Nor can he say it out loud.
It comes out as a great belch
of grey smoke from the mouth
or a vomiting forth of
ill-digested bones and gristle.

He pleads for attention. We hurry on by.
This public scene – there is no charge for admission –
has been going on for years.
We are tired of his antics,
we tight-arsed lovers.

Gottlieb's Sleeping Habits

Gottlieb is never awake when I am awake.
I stare at him down there in the shadows.
I even prod him with a stick.
He never stirs.

Even when I read to him,
he snores on until the ceiling trembles,
and especially so when it is
The Bird With Three Eyes –

during which I dance and I dance
around the room in front of him,
suitably bedizened, suitably frenetic,
coloured chalks tight-gripped in my hand.

At such moments as these,
he is exquisitely lost to me.

Gottlieb's Bone-Idleness

It was only on the day of your death
that you returned to me.
You had been absent for so long
that I had grown quite accustomed
to living without you.

And then you presented yourself in front of me
like a fresh-plucked daisy,
fragrant, in your cerements.
I did not hesitate
to embrace you.

I showed you the world
and how it had grown apart from you.
You nodded your disapproval.
I asked you why
you had not intervened.

Idleness, bone-idleness, you commented.

Gottlieb's Insistence

No goodbye is ever quite sufficient.
You are never not here with me.
Even when I burn my memories,
You rise up again, you filthy Phoenix.
Even when I slam the door on you,
you are cooking eggs by candlelight in the kitchen.
This bedroom has the lingering smell of you.
This mirror has the look of you
even when I stare deep into my own
dark and hollowed sockets.

Gottlieb Is Such a Tease

Gottlieb has his way with me.
Every morning he has
his small and wheedling way with me.
I say: ease over a little.
Or: turn your back on me.
Does he do as he is told?

When we walk out arm in arm
to examine the stream's soft chuckle,
we are all sweet whistles and crisp laughter.
The thunderous applause of demons
does not apply any more.
The sky will not collapse on us today.

Gottlieb Dreams and Takes the Air

Gottlieb's dreams arrive in multiples –
death in the kangaroo park,
the tulip's slow, hard swallow,
corpulence, dissolved in tears,
god, again, beating his hollow log.

Gottlieb takes the air to be rid of it all.
Bat-flurries welcome him.
Houses jostle for attention.
Summer's slow boom leaves him reeling.
Everything, he comments, is *almost* or *maybe*.

Gottlieb's Questions

If not nowhere, where else could you be going?

The questions follow Gottlieb
like fairy lights strung down a street.

Is it the usual, my dear?
Could you ask her to crack open the opportunities?
Are there miles and miles still to be reckoned with?
Does the street signage lack conviction?
Is your best friend newly coffin-confined?
Can there be good luck without acute disappointment?
Will the mules be ready at the point of exhaustion?

Gottlieb's Several Deaths, At Least One Magnificent

Gottlieb has died before,
he informs us,
with a confidence bordering
on the defiant.

Self-wounding was a cause
of one such death.
The reason, please?
Shame.

Another death invoked
the charge of heroism –
rescuing a nurse maid,
harried by coyotes,
from the upper limbs of
a eucalyptus tree.

The nurse maid survived
to leave flowers on his grave,
repeatedly.

His best of deaths, he says,
is not to be spoken of.

Instead, he draws a circle in the sand,
drives a stick into its middle,
and touches the stick's end, lightly,
with a bloodied finger's end, his own.

Truly impressive.

The Slowness of Gottlieb

Gottlieb's hours are
trudging-slow today,
so slow in fact
that the minutes seem like years,
and each second is devoted to
a close observation of
the painstaking creation of
the Pyramid of Cheops,
stone by rolled stone.

When he raises his dust-choked
eyes from the desert,
he sees the bagel in front of him,
his breakfast bagel from long, long ago –
(perhaps a minute?) –
patiently waiting to be slow-rended
by the deep, sub-aquatic flow
of the ends of his fingers.

The Mysteries of Gottlieb's Brain

Gottlieb's brain does not slow
when spoken to.
Instead, it is a street light
blinking on

at that poignant crepuscular moment when
the whores slink out from
the back alleys of Paris –
all glittery-tall and minty-breathed –

to deceive us all into believing that
the entire world is in our hands,
and that there will never be an end
to all this restlessness.

Gottlieb's Relative Insignificance

Gottlieb's makeshift hours
are compounded of lust,
grievance and small-talk.
That is all there is of him.
The sack is upended.

No wonder you
missed him that day
when he called on you again and again,
ringing your bell,
hammering down on the knocker.

When you walked out to take a stroll,
he was waiting there, standing in front of you.
You took him for a house mite, a pavement nothing.
You crushed him with the sole of your shoe
without a second's hesitation.

Gottlieb's Current Predicament

There is less of Gottlieb
than you might imagine, much less.
You thought him full-grown?
Let me disappoint you.
He is a barren field,
a yawning dearth
in a land of plenty.

In the streets of laughter,
his is the risible piping squeak
of the mouse, quick-lifted,
and twirled by the tail.

At the table, his is the smallest portion,
the meanest of the small-talk,
and, needless to say, he sits in
the most footling of chairs
because, moment by moment,
he is dwindling down to nothing.

Quite deservedly, of course.

Gottlieb's Unexpected Arrival

At the moment when loneliness engulfs,
Gottlieb arrives to take our measure –
a glitter of sea spray,
a columnar leaning of shadow,
the tallest of our exaggerations.

How we embrace him,
offering him comforts by the fistful –
sweets to be sucked on,
stories to be pecked apart,
lovers by the sackful.

Gottlieb and the Ridiculous

The days swing back and forth –
laughter, tears, indifference.
Gottlieb walks amongst us,
whispering his words of comfort,

setting the bottles upright,
hauling his waters of healing
from wells unsuspected.
He is never not here amongst us.

We live amongst the ridiculous,
and Gottlieb pardons us for that,
soothing the brow of one forever feverish,
stanching the slow drip-drip of venom.

We do as we have always done.
We respect him as one cloud amongst many,
and we also choose to ignore him
because he is as ancient as this bench

on which we squat and wait
for the world to terminate,
peaceably enough
in this troubled season.

Gottlieb's Makeshift World

Gottlieb's is a makeshift world.
He loves us for all that we are not.
When we hesitate to speak of him,
he climbs upon the garden fence
and delivers his daily oration.
So many words! Such chastening sentiments!
The news is from everywhere, he says.
The last breath is always ours to take.

Gottlieb the Conjuror

Make of it what you will.
I have no reason to tease you.
Gottlieb comes and goes – that's his wont,
a will o' the wisp, the least snatch of a madrigal.

Make of it what you will.
His name can be picked apart.
The goodness is all his,
the lack is ours, alone.

Make of him what you will –
from the shadows to the uplands
he flits and roams, does Gottlieb,
our conjuror of worlds.

The Quality of Gottlieb's Sleeping

Gottlieb sleeps in his sanctuary
with the mice and the carpet beetles.
Do not disturb him.

He is thinking, reverentially,
of all that Gott told him
of how one day

he would grow and grow
until the entire world
was consumed by him.

That big! That impressive!
Meanwhile, let him snore here
just out of earshot, thankfully.

The Masterfulness of Gottlieb

When Gottlieb takes a step,
we all follow.
We are his pupils.
He is our teacher.

When Gottlieb opens his mouth to bellow,
we open ours too –
there is so much
breath in the world!

When Gottlieb eats of the earth's bounty,
we are encouraged to gather the crumbs from his table
from which to create a feast of our own.
Such plentifulness! Such generosity!

When the mask of Gottlieb
slips away from each of us,
it is then that the blood flows,
the blood and all these random tears.

All Praise to the Name of Gottlieb

Gottlieb is our name to conjure with.
Every day we take it to school.
Every day we smooth it out across our desks.

Some of us produce fireworks, smashing the classroom windows!

Others precipitate a low drone,
a little like a power drill in the wall of a distant room.

Yet others bound along with the letters,
making odd, pantomimic gestures.

There is just no telling where his name will lead us.

My At-Oneness with Gottlieb

Gottlieb has denied me everything.
He removed my heart with surgical precision.
He twisted off my fingers with a single deft turn.
From my eyes he made a gelatinous soup of sorts.

With my voice he gave the sea birds a song.
From my feet he created a sculpture entitled
       Determination, Part 2.
With my arms he flailed at the air, ridding it of all confusion.
Into my mouth he inserted a posy of sweet williams.

Of my hair he fashioned – after long hours of labour –
carpet slippers to ease away the pain of his ancient bunions.
Gottlieb and I are as one now.
I am all that he has become.

Gottlieb's Most Magical Instrument

From all the labours of all our lives,
Gottlieb has fashioned an undying instrument –
a little like a tuba crossed – very crossed! –
with a piano, a xylophone and a violin...

How we warm to the din,
carrying our weightless legs
down the pinched, twisty streets
of the Old City,

bringing nursemaids, twin paps hanging,
to their windows,
causing the crones to blush or to smile
from beneath the coping of
their moth-eaten lambswool bonnets,

forcing even the beeriest of men
to run and to run on their tottery legs
until they fall, altogether,
in a single, uproarious heap.

What music Gottlieb must have shared with them
to bring such happiness about!

Light, Gottlieb?

Is there much light here, Gottlieb?
Call it light if you wish.
I know it as svelte memories, cartoonish pie-throwings,
filthy delvings amongst the nows and the thens.

Is there much dark here, Gottlieb?
When will you put an end to all these questionings?
I could give you a stick to tap your way forward,
a straight, stiff serpent of a bowl-me-along...

The Triumph of Gottlieb's Recklessness

Whose house is yours, Gottlieb? I ask him.
We are standing together,
wind-buffeted, dreaming,
on the pinnacle of the temple.

He indicates: seven villas in the suburbs,
three mid-town condos,
a palazzo in the foothills amongst the lemon groves,
and several terraces for the working man.

When he throws himself off at my suggestion,
he lands, to a thin fritter of applause,
at the mid-point of a sturdy Tudor chimney pot,
one of several he recently acquired at auction.

Gottlieb Explicates Himself

Gottlieb stands in the sun-kissed courtyard, arms akimbo,
carefully picking apart his own intricacies.

I am not the Many within the One, he explains.
I am both the Many *and* the One.
He makes a violent circling motion with his hands,
as if unravelling a ball of wool at high speed.

I am not that which comes after.
I am continuous.
I have never begun and I shall never end.

See this hand...
(He stretches out his hand.)
This is the weapon which felled the kingdom,
pulverised armies, blasted mountains, and,
having done so,
neatly assembled them again,
and to such an extent
that the After resembled the Before
to the last and most minute particular...

He narrowed his eyes just then.
We were sucked into his eyes,
and we are still there,
musing upon a particular release date,
albeit trustingly.

How Gottlieb Enables Us

Gottlieb has released us from the shadow of our days.
We run like children, arms flailing,
singing from the rooftops of our mouths.

Our bodies have never known such airiness.
We are lighter than a breath.
When we touch, we bounce off, spinning.

Then he sits each one of us down
on a hard stool
for a lesson or two –

the division of night from day, death from life,
cold poverty from the glitter of abundance,
loose talk from the hammered nail of a truth.

He shows us the corpse
of a small animal or two.
We choke on the stink of it all.

Gottlieb's Words

We are all sojourners in a foreign land.

Those are Gottlieb's words,
stolen from his mouth.

And now I offer them around,
to you and to you.

When we lie warm in our beds,
when we eat pie at the table,

when we congratulate each other
upon the great success of the wheat crop
or the bringing in, steaming, of the Paschal Lamb,

when we shower each other
with the gift of goodness
or the goodness of gifts in abundance,

when we speak well of our neighbours,
and refuse to countenance hatred,

when the night sky protects us
and the sunlight bathes us,

when all things seems good to us,
from the first dew drop to the last mouse dropping,

it is then that we must remember Gottlieb's words:
we are all sojourners in a foreign land.

The Importance of Gottlieb's Interventions

When Gottlieb gives too little praise to the morning,
we open our windows to drizzle and grey skies.

When Gottlieb fails to give thanks to the bakers
                      for their night-hours' toil,
the bread comes out black and hard.
We break our teeth on it.

When Gottlieb is not present at the birth of a child,
wild cries go up from the newborn.
The mother cowers in her bed beneath bloodied sheets.

When Gottlieb does not shake the hands of the steeplejack,
the clock tower on the village green begins to sag and to lean,
                                              alarmingly.

When Gottlieb does not pray for us all,
we race through our lives like blind machines
which have lost all control of their destinies.

What Gottlieb Did

All grown together, fitly, neatly...

Each finger screwed onto the plumped palm,
without seam, without join.

Head placed atop
as a swivelling watchtower for the spirit.

Feet bottom-most,
to steady, carry forward,
and even to loiter on a corner,
of an evening, quizzically,
when the light is falling.

Organs well stuffed out of sight,
working ceaselessly, night, day, night,
without order, without instructions from the body,
as if to know is to work and to work is to know.

Who made it all like this?
Why, Gottlieb, we cry,
he alone did it!

Gottlieb's All-Encompassing Love

Has anyone warmed to a brick
as Gottlieb has warmed to a brick,
caressing it, wrapping it in several blankets,
speaking soft, soothing words into its tiny, wrinkly fissures?

Has anyone seen such brightness in an old tin can,
weeping over it, pointing, repeatedly pointing,
and then re-filling it with cooling water
for the sheer pleasure of drinking from it again?

Has anyone ever loved a broken stool
in the way that Gottlieb has loved a broken stool,
setting it upright, devising a new broken stool song
so that the broken heart of the broken stool

is quickened back to life, and sees itself again
as that new stool, so upright, so proud,
gleaming so brightly in the furniture store window,
obsessively counting and re-counting its four straight legs?

Gottlieb Intercedes For Us All in Our Extreme Fragility

Those visits I never made, again and again,
to those who needed me most,
today Gottlieb told me *he* had made them instead.
How did he find the time?
Who gave him the addresses?

Those poems I never wrote in his praise,
always so many and all of them so long,
he received them after all, he explained.
And when I asked him whether I had written them well,
better than most, he shrugged, half-smiling.

This messy fistful of broken promises,
I shall offer them to Gottlieb.
He will know what to do with them.

In the Darkest of Nights, Gottlieb...

In the darkest of nights,
I stand tall, beamed down upon
by Gottlieb's sunshine.

When the rains carry me away,
and I watch my body drifting
to the very edge
of the steepest and most deep plunging
of Canadian waterfalls,
Gottlieb sweeps me up
in the flat of his hand,
so deftly that I applaud him inwardly
even as my body is still quaking.

When the most extreme fits of melancholy are upon me,
and my soul fills with fogs of disappointment
and anger and jealousy and self-disgust and general disarray,
Gottlieb twists off the stopper
of the smallest vial of healing balm
ever to be held in a palm
and lets it drip, drip, drip
down onto my maddened, manicked skull
until it becomes a wide-flung casement
giving onto the calmness of a summer's lake,
readied, breeze-combed, for swift, bold kayaking.

The Nature of Gottlieb

Gottlieb walks in a certain way,
side-on, visible yet invisible,
in short: inimitable.

Gottlieb's voice is the rarest of sounds:
between our hearings, we hear it;
between our speakings, when all has fallen silent,
its whisperings interpose themselves.

Gottlieb writes as only Gottlieb writes.
We read his words without seeing them.
In fact, we have read them through and through
even before he has written them.

What Gottlieb Does For Us

Gottlieb finds what we lose.
Gottlieb repairs what we broke.
Gottlieb speaks the words we forgot to speak.
Gottlieb takes the journeys we meant to take.

Gottlieb apologises for our carelessness.
Gottlieb scrubs the evil from our palms.
Gottlieb teaches us the manners of a gentleman.
Gottlieb teaches us the scamperings of an imp.

Gottlieb never loses track of us.
Gottlieb always quick-turns and breathes into our face.
Gottlieb is never knowingly absent from us.
Gottlieb presents himself, variously,
    as pavement, bucket or rain.

Gottlieb as Guru

Is there a hope, a last hope,
for all of us?

Did you not say
we were beyond that now,
on the wrong side of the outer limits,
facing nowhere?

Gottlieb says: wait.
He sits in his chair and he calls to us.
He closes the shutters.
He lights the candles, one, two, three,
with a degree of slow ceremony.

He invites us to extend our down-turned palms,
fingers evenly spread.
We extend our down-turned palms,
fingers evenly spread.
He asks us to breathe,
to scoop in the air and then breathe,
to the last rag of breath in our lungs.

This headiness begins to mean something.
We are all smiling faintly.
We are facing back again,
in the general direction of home,
in the general direction of hope.

Gottlieb

Who makes the pity to flow?
Who opens the vein, and makes the pity to flow?

Who gives life where there was no life?
Who breathes on a seed beside the road?
Who makes this tree wide enough to be given
           a fond embrace?

Who gives this new babe its furious parpings,
its bunched fists,
its wild rockings from side to side?

Who tells this mother to lie so still there,
pale and contented, smiling upward,
when the man goes, and does not return,
and has not provided?

Who is this ridiculous power-sprinkler of hope?

Gottlieb's Warning

Are there lessons in duty to be learned?
Are there buildings, flat on their backs,
ready to be set upright again?

Are there clouds to be tidied away
into the corners of the sky?
Are their raging rivers to be spoken to firmly?

Are there people, side-on in their beds,
craving, in tiny, helpless voices,
to stand tall in their slippers?

Are there moments of generosity still to come?
Are there bands to be heard, hands to be shaken,
mouths to be kissed, gifts to be exchanged?

Is this cityscape of rubble
that I see ahead of me
merely Gottlieb's warning?

In short, have all the mountebanks now gone away?

Upon the Nature of Gottlieb's General Availability

Not the latest hour.
Not the latest possible hour.
Not the hour when Gottlieb arrives.
Not the hour when Gottlieb leaves again.

Not the hour when Gottlieb is too busy to be spoken to.
Not the hour when Gottlieb is thronged by well-wishers.
Not the hour when Gottlieb kneels to pray in the sanctuary.
Not the hour when Gottlieb dispenses gifts to the poor.

Not the hour when a notice reports of Gottlieb's absence.
Not the hour when Gottlieb strays alone through woodland,
feeding the birds, communing with the smallest creature.
Some other occasion, perhaps. Yes.

Gottlieb's Idea of an Adventure

I have ventured, strong legs forward-going,
into this wilderness of sorts,
where the sands rise neck-high,
and there is precious little conversation.

Who is with me here?
It is hard to say.
Just the two or three of us?
Or perhaps it is seven, eight or more.

All energy is expended in the pushing on, on, on.
The passage of days is not counted.
We have sand, sand, sand in our eyes.
Sand to eat. Sand for a pillow.

Gottlieb

Each day I used to say:
I covet your presence a little more.
Soon you will be with me.
Soon you will be the near perfect
embodiment of my imaginings.

I fashioned you from letters of the alphabet.
Days and days I worked with you on the floor,
pushing you around, murmuring over the sequences.
There was such strong anticipation
mingled with anxiety and pleasure!

Your consonants stuck in my throat.
Your vowels caused me to rise to the ceiling.
Now that I have you here,
I almost believe that your name
is a guarantee of your presence here with me.

Gottlieb Displaces Us

Gottlieb has sealed us in this box
and set us aside.
We wait patiently now.
We do not complain.
We do not drum on the lid.
Neither do we sing our songs of praise.

Gottlieb has sealed us in this box
for reasons known only to himself.
We were going about our days,
tossing vegetables from hand to hand,
fetching water from the well,
keeping a guarded eye on the horizon line.

It was then that he plucked us up, one by one,
and set us down in this box, side by side,
like a perfect fit of white dominoes
with black dots for eyes.
We did not think to complain as our bodies were hoisted.
Some even enjoyed the aerial manoeuvrings.

Is it a matter of days?
Have our beards grown over-long?
Do we feel comfortable, wedged in here,
side by side, arms stretched long?
Is this a torment then
or the gateway to Paradise?

Gottlieb's Antics

Gottlieb's restless pacings
cause the earth to tremble.
We cower in our bunkers,
praying that he will lose interest,
that a new star in the firmament
will wink and bedazzle him.

Gottlieb's vile bellowings
shoot such pains
through the inner ear
that the beds in the emergency wards
are full of heads
writhing and ringing.

Gottlieb's strict instructions –
what to do and when,
where to go and how –
cause such general dismay
that we burn his effigy in the public square:
an Angel of Mercy bowed low in mock-humility.

Gottlieb's Succour

I am so small today.
Only Gottlieb makes me
six feet tall in my stockinged feet.

I whimper and I cry
in the corner of the kitchen.
I have spilled hot tea on my tie.
I have mislaid my work suit.

Only Gottlieb can sweep in
and deal with these things for me.
Only Gottlieb can help to dress
my trembling body.

The rain on my face
induces a misery so exquisite
that I cannot leave the house.

Gottlieb walks beside me,
every step of the way,
man-handling the brolly.

The Pursuit of Gottlieb

When I call, he does not listen.
Wherever I look, he is not to be found.
The streets are swept clean of all trace of him.
The clouds, unheeding, idle by.

There is no talk of him in the cafés.
The food has no savour of his goodness.
The water is bland
in the way that only water can be.

When I note his name down in my book,
it does not come alive for me
in the way that other names come alive – yours, for example.
No matter how many times I speak it out loud,
nothing resonates within me.

Have I offended him in some way?
Was I wrong to believe that we meant
             something to each other?
Was that first appeal he made to me
some nonsense of a scrambled brain?
Has it all been so much base trickery?

The Triumphal Campaign
from: The First Book of Gottlieb, Ch. 7, verses 9–63

Gottlieb sent down his army,
all bayonets bristling.
He laid waste to the villages,
burning houses, stealing cattle, saffron, bullion,
wrenching large joints of meat from the freezer.

He plucked out the most comely of the teenagers,
idling over her throughout the night hours.
By dawn's bright sunlight,
he removed head from body, cleanly.
She yawped too much in her fitful sleep for his liking.

The enemy's greatest warriors were brought to him,
one by one, trembling, naked,
for careful inspection.
He de-testicled them,
then pushed them behind the barn
to be out of earshot of their mewling.

Gottlieb marched into the city
behind a flurry of banners,
to roars of welcome
from the mob that surged to glimpse him.
We come in peace! the soldiery cried.
He nodded along as he swayed from side to side,
gently surveying, saying nothing.

Gottlieb, the Final Credits

Once he dealt well by us.
Our skies were of the utmost clarity.
Our people walked the public byways in peace.

His was a name to conjure with.
We called it an august name.
We sang it in our sleep.

Now all this has changed.
Night has fallen. Winter cold descends on us.
We shiver. We feel unmanned.

We have passed beyond all welcoming.
Let us bury him now.
Let us stamp on his grave.

Gottlieb's is a stranger's grave.

The Death of a Mother

She

When she did not wake up,
I did not speak to her.
When she did not talk to me,
I did not ask her a question.

When I did not kiss her,
she did not embrace me.
Why is she gone from me?
What has happened to her?

I know what it is to see her,
I know what it is to be with her.
And now I am not seeing her.
And now I am no longer with her.

And yet still I do see her.
And yet still I do speak to her.
And yet still I do walk with her –
as far as the doorstep, for example, where we both sit down.

No one can stop us being there.
I can sit with her just as long as she wishes.
And she wishes a long long time.
She wishes that even when she is absent.

When she is no longer my mother here,
she is still always my mother.

Can It Be Right?

Can it be right? I said
when it rained.
Can it be right ever again?
And it kept on raining.

Is this the way things are?
I said to the shops that morning.
The shops were the same old places,
as were the people, the wet pavements.

Am I myself? I asked me.
I saw nothing in the mirror.
I saw her face in the mirror.
She had stepped in front of me.

I touched her nose with my finger.
It was cold as a mirror is always cold.

All Sleep Has Died

All sleep has died.
I cannot make it happen.
I cannot close my eyes.
There is only this staring.

And with staring goes looking –
hard, into her face,
asking her why, why, why,
why always so many bottles.

All sleep has died.
There are only these questions,
one behind another, always here,
always and forever another.

Where you have taken yourself.
Why there is such a silence.
Why I am leaving this house
when my feet choose to lead me.

Can I Make You See Me?

How much am I to make of you now?
Should I draw pictures of my memories?
Should I write down the words you said to me?
Will you speak to me again, huskily?

How much am I to make of you now?
Should I try to follow you?
Or should I just sit here on my own
and talk to you, very, very quietly,

so that no one else hears us,
and no one interrupts us,
and no one says that we cannot,
and that it is impossible anyway?

No Longer There

A nail fell out of my hand.
I was holding it, and then it fell.
The window too, that disappeared.
It was only the clear blue sky beyond.

Your words, they too stopped coming,
such noisy words, and in full flow,
filling all of the kitchen,
and then spilling down into the garden,

they stopped all of a sudden,
and when I looked back to find you
at the beginning of your words,
your mouth was no longer there for me.

What Has Happened?

What has happened to the days?
What has happened to their fullness?
They have grown very thin.
They have grown very small.

What has happened to my life?
Why are my fingers not twisting?
Why do I hold them so still,
as if they are not very useful?

What has happened to my mouth?
Yesterday it was full of sounds.
Now there is only air inside my mouth,
very still air, very slow to be stirring.

My You

You had shrunk
to a tiny part of you,
mother, my mother,
when I found you.

It was not all of you,
what I saw there on the floor.
You would not have wanted it
to be all of you.

It was not what you
would have showed me of yourself,
had you had the strength
that moment to choose

because you also loved me so much
in all your sadness and all your helplessness,
and you would have wanted to show me
something of your laughter and your hopefulness,

something of another you who
had also been you,
and that too
is my you, mother.

And all of this is true.

Death's Moment

When the past came back,
so strong, so vivid, so embraceable,
I took it for a nowness so loveable,
that no one could stir me back to consciousness.

Nothing Has Happened

Nothing has happened here again.
I wake up and nothing has happened.
You are still on the floor,
and I cannot budge you.

No one can budge you.
You will always be there for me,
even when they have removed you
to another room,

you will always be there,
and I will always be standing over you,
not knowing what to do,
at the very edge of my life, peering over,

and pleading for you to tell me
what to do with your body down there,
pleading for you to hold me,
and to turn me back towards the door

by which I entered to find you,
pleading for you to lead me
back into the garden,
your arm on my arm,

and then seeing the bus arriving,
and running to catch it,
back, back to my babyhood,
with me in your arms, always.

Chosen Words

I see more of you now
that I no longer see you at all.
I see you when I close my eyes.
I see you throughout the night,

doing things for me, large and small –
packing up sandwiches, picking up books,
speaking to me alone
when I barely listen to you.

It is these words I miss the most,
the words I did not listen to,
I hear the sound of them on the air,
unmistakably yours, carefully bottled for me,

and handed over so casually
for me to set aside, so carelessly.
Each one of them I pick up now.
I re-run your words,

the large and the small,
this word for me alone,
that other one I chose to ignore,
and all so carefully bottled for me.

My Brick

A brick is like any other brick.
A brick is only good for a wall.
No one stares at a brick.
No one cares for a brick at all.

I set this brick aside.
I kept it by my bed.
And now it has gone.
Someone has found a use for it.

You say it was only a brick.
A brick is good for a wall.
No one looks at a brick.
No one cares for a brick at all.

I set this brick aside.
I kept it by my bed.
And now it has gone.
Someone has found a need for it.

A brick is like any other brick.
A brick is only good for a wall.
No one stares at a brick.
No one cares for a brick at all.

The Scarf

This knitted scarf I keep for you,
hung on this door,
curled up in this box,
straggled across this bed
behind my window.

All your love for me
was in the way your fingers worked
to make it – all those loopings and twistings,
arounds and in-betweens,
inch by inch of it, coming into being.

My fear, most of all, is that I shall lose you
when I lose this scarf on the bus,
in the street, at school, at a party,
everyone else in the world
being so careless
about what it really means,
the weight and the warmth of it
curled about my neck, to love and protect me,
my fear that, once it is gone, you will be gone from me.

And yet you will not, I know that for sure
because you are more than this scarf.
My scarf of all my memories
will always hang about my neck –
how the scarf itself felt,
how your fingers worked,
how you smiled at me when you gave it.
No one can erase all that.

The Muffled Light

That Yellow Light

There is no clear seeing any more.
All seeing is rubbed and smudged,
as if through a fog on a winter's night,
driving for hours at a time,
on a snaking road, climbing,

so hazardous, so unrelenting...
And on we drive as we ask:
will we ever arrive at journey's end,
will we see beside the road
the muffled glare of that yellow light?

The Healing
for Jesse

On an unknown day
there was a covert
in which you hid yourself away
for just as long as you needed.

There sleep took hold of you,
and rocked you for hour after hour
until the healing was over,
and then once again you walked free.

No Telling

There is no way of telling
how a word becomes a book,
becomes a kingdom,
with its peoples, its arguments,
its multiple uncertainties.

All we ever know
is how it starts in us
as a flicker, an intuition,
the quick upstart of
a bird from a post

just beyond the eye's
furthest corner.
You turn, of a sudden,
as if knowing something.
You lunge to catch at it.

The Parcel

I would have had you stay, you know that,
but you, with all your threadbare garments,
were always slipping away.

And now you have gone for good.
I have turned out these cupboards. Nothing.
I have walked these streets. Nowhere to be seen.

What then became of you?
Were you alive before I was born?
Did you prosper, mightily, after my death?

Such questions! There is no way of telling.
Who makes a manageable parcel these days
out of all this nothingness?

The Sage in the Gulley

Far beyond the outer limits of this kingdom,
there is an open gulley where an old man sleeps
of foulest temper.

No one knows why he rages.
No one knows why he left us here.
No one knows when he will return.

All we know is that until he returns,
hesitant, in sackcloth and ashes,
scuffing his feet as he goes,

randomly spitting in all directions,
nothing will be right with us again,
and no new children will be born to us.

My Ever Sweet Familiar

Who is to blame for all of this?
Surely not you again.
You were innocent on that day,

shredding paper into yet smaller pieces
as you blithely welcomed the rising sun
with a song – as was always your way.

I say then that you were blameless,
and that the face of you I see everywhere,
raised up high or spiked or trampled underfoot,

is not your face, not even similar.
Are you not still long gone,
my wraith, my ever sweet familiar?

A Stink of Meat

The trencher board
now stinks of meat.
Dispose of it.
Your lips are stretched
too tight for my favours.
Fetch me a blade, a rag,
and a bundle of excuses.

Otherwise, the day looks
fine, winsome, airy.
The scuts are all lopped,
and the music apposite.
Summon the rest of that
rag-tag-and-bobtail lot
to the banquet.

The Past Comes Later

The rest – like the past – came later,
long after the flowering time,
you must understand,
but, all told, things
are much as they were,
and I hear you clearly,

here, as ever, hour by hour,
on the hour,
when the noise has receded,
and the bells have reminded me
to desist from tolling
in opposition.

I do get ahead of myself these days.
It is in my nature
never quite to understand.
And yours too, I seem to recall,
though somewhat doubtfully,
and with some hesitation.

The Clap

Were your eyes taken by what you saw,
and, if so, how far?
There is much that is invisible here,
in this hollow between the mountains.

We have spent days drifting and talking,
and remaining sullenly silent.
There is much still to come, we are told,
we tell ourselves, much to be taken by

beyond the next level
when the snow gentles to a flurry,
and the passes once again fall open
with the faintest of faint clap of hands.

The Tragic Loss
of the Harmonies of Heaven

You have made so little
of the little that was made of you.
And yet I do envy you your forebodings:
the crack in the door grows ever larger;
you gather your night things about you,
tooth brush, soft cap, copper spoon.
Who robbed you so early
of the harmonies of heaven?

The Next Way Forward

This way across and through
cannot be described too carefully.
At the crossroads, throw a right as you might
toss a gift to a friend neglected overlong.

When reaching the junction
enveloped in cobwebs and mist,
shout a little to dissipate
the worst of it.

At the second stop sign,
argue against its authority:
for whom exactly are you stopping?
And on whose orders?

When you reach the cottage,
finger the damp – or otherwise –
of the thatch. If all is good and ready,
strike then your match.

The Oldness of Now

All that happened then
is happening again.
Have you not noticed?
The sea has returned to the land
with such enthusiasm,

floating our most beloved things
across such stretched grey levels
of watery vastness,
as if paper, cardboard, wood,
and even ceramic bowls
were nothing but dreams of themselves
forever dissolving...

Yet we must go after, chasing them
in all our foolishness,
shrieking, grasping.
Stop. Turn back.
Accept that this must be so.
Our moment is over.
This nowness is so long ago.

He, Frédéric Chopin

He, Chopin, had often bad-dreamed,
in those hours of idling sadness,
that the *chaise longue*
standing pert and four-square
at the opposite end
of the *piano nobile*
to He with his piano,

would in time become his equal
in its social presence,
its good graces
and (one can only say it,
albeit with some reluctance),
its pianistical panache.

Not that he had ever wished
to contemplate a rival.
Nor had he ever quite truly believed
that a piece of mute furniture,
even one raised up by
its presence there on castors
(just three of them just then)
could ever be the equal
of a tremendous flurry of
his bedazzling Polish fingers
with their decidedly French accents.

And so he waited until such time
as the upholsterer, small, quick and Italian,
should come with his bolts of fabric
(several metres), harlequin-patterned,
his thin, fine braiding –

in all its shrieking gold of King Midas –
and his machine with its
stab, stab, stab of bright-shining needles...

And now it was all done and dusted
and alive in its sun-struck, afternoon moment,
and the two were being introduced at last
in front of a crowd of, say,
sixty or seventy of the most
puffed up and pampered of Old Paris,
with their crocodile smiles
and their delicate glasses,
which tinkled so gently
against their finger rings...

And when the *chaise longu*e rolled up to him,
as any human might do,
with a certain swagger,
in all the prideful sheen of
its re-fashioned surface,
He found himself almost inclined
to defer as he sat down at the piano
and tinkered with his notes
which, in time, would become
the most tremendous crescendo,
and one played, perhaps,
in bitter homage to
his latest, newest, and finest of rivals.

Passing Through

Lightly, as if on tiptoe,
he passed through the vestibule,
travelling airily
he knew not where,
seeing only a menial light ahead of him,
of a candle, he guessed...

Not so. It was the light of
every new day's dawning,
at the very hint of its
first beginnings,
and it lifted him up

until his feet barely
touched any longer
that cold parquet surface
across which it had been his wont
to wander at whim
until just this morning.

Any Single Passing Moment
to Paul Verlaine

le ciel est par dessus le toit
si bleu, si calme...

You would never have guessed it.
It would have been too improbable,
too simple in its earthly perfections...

To take a roof such as this one,
and a single bird passing over,
in a hurry to be gone,
is more than enough
for any single passing moment.

It was – and it is.
We return to it,
lingering over,
the profoundest of books,
openable at any and every page,
which is, of course, always this one.

Lightness Is All

You spoke to me
as if whispering into your sleeve.
Where are we going? you said,
barely gesturing with your head.

I looked up and around.
No one was looking.
In a crowded room,
no one knows, no one sees.
Always too much of everything.

And so we left,
through the bathroom window,
both us being so light, so slight,
so unencumbered.

Counting Our Steps
or: *walking a little of the 28A from the house,*
having turned right at the bottom of the drive,
away from the spillway...

for Ed, and all he was to us

Season by season, things change and change again.
This morning, early to avoid the sun,
in fact, a shade past seven o'clock,
down the drive we go, easy does it,
for corn silk and day lilies beside the road...
And in such profusion!
See them?
That is what we call them in these parts.
I know that you don't, not necessarily.
You like to hear these pretty flower names,
am I not correct about that?
They can seem so exotic to you Brits,
just as yours can to us.

Walk slowly in the direction of the traffic.
That is the rule of the road.
Why should we hurry?
Who or what are we trying to gain on?
We are keeping pace with no one
but our three good selves,
side by side on relatively level ground
(except when it gently goes up or down),
saying intermittently this and that,
in order to confirm our friendship if you like,
and also to catch up
because there is much of that to be done....
Is it three years or not?

That is a lot!
Yes, I knew I could not be far wrong...

I can tell you little or much just as you please,
and you can listen or tune me out.
I am here for you.
I am still that same friend
who has always prepared you
your morning coffee,
in the kitchen upstairs
(when you still slept there,
before our son vacated his room
and moved to Kingston)
overlooking the lake
(before the tree growth obscured it)
with a degree of methodical ceremoniousness,
as is my wont, I am sure you will agree.

And it is I who am leading you now
on this morning walk
which I habitually do when I am not in the city,
and you are accompanying me on it
because you have chosen so to do
on this lovely July morning,
which is only the second of your visit.
Yes, I am counting!
No stranger is with us today,
though one could be welcome
if he or she happened along,
which is extremely unlikely.

You know that sign well
because it has always amused you:
SLOW CHURCH ZONE.

Remember you asked us once
whether we ever attended,
forgetting that we are good, New York,
non-observant Jews?
How we all laughed!

They've got family living around,
those Living Word people,
quite some community these days,
young and old... That's their car there,
at the end of Huckleberry Lane,
all made up with cinder these days –
makes it easier to drive up –
with the kids jumping out and staring.
I always wave back when they wave.
They're no bother. Take a look.
They're friendly enough.
There's space enough in front of the church
to park all their cars on a Sunday.
They know their God wouldn't allow them
to block up the road, and so they don't.
The congregation's just grown and grown and grown.

The red flag is up on the mail box.
That always impresses you, I know,
that the mail man is looking out
to satisfy our every postal need,
driveway by driveway, box by box.

My daily walk is usually about eight thousand steps
here or in the city. I try to keep it the same.
There, it's a left out of the building,
crossing Amsterdam,
and then directly up 85th and into the park,

where I can pick up my reservoir walk,
and then curve gently back,
all very satisfying and really quite easy
now I'm so used to it.
And it's very good for me.
I know that for a fact
without the doctor even saying.
Who needs a doctor when you can self-diagnose
with the internet...

If I wanted to make it a little longer
by taking in breakfast out,
I would go past our building
and down to the corner of Broadway,
to French Roast for coffee
and two eggs over easy on sourdough perhaps.
We can do that when you're back.
Just remind me.
I'd be happy to show you.

You see all those vehicles over there?
Beside the house, in front, behind...
That guy's in lumber.
Count the trucks for yourself –
eight if I'm not mistaken.
No, we don't know him,
except to nod to.
He's a good man.
I've never heard any different.

Do we care that we've lost the view
of the reservoir from the deck?
Sure. We care a lot.
There's only so much

of your life you can spend delighting in
the wonder of hummingbirds at the feeder,
that miracle of hovering
as they dip at the sugary drink,
the gauzy blur of those near invisible wings...
It was always so great of an evening
letting your eye drift across all that water
to the Catskills beyond...
Do they care a jot about what we want,
the City authorities?
Do they lose sleep over the fact that
they haven't cut the trees back in years,
and when we ask if we can do it
because it is we who suffer,
bark at us: no we cannot?
Go fuck you is the answer!

Where the shadow falls in a stripe
across the road, that's where we turn back,
that's my marker at this hour.
So here goes. Ready?
There are no cars...
You don't have to do it tomorrow
if you're not up in time, you know.
We know all about jet-lag,
how tired and hazy it makes you.
On the other hand,
with my duck paddle of a walk,
you may think it agreeably easy
to walk with an old guy who's
always so slow and so steady.
Plus there's much that I still haven't told you!

The Long, Wise Sleep

Sleep long before night comes
with all its hours of wakefulness,
needling questions, illusions dispelled,
the horror of the truths of things.

Sleep long before night comes
with all its closed-box certainties,
the having-beens, the long-since-gones,
to grope is the essence of night-wandering.

Sleep long before night comes,
and then again a little more,
beyond the night, the final sleep,
the long, wise sleep of nothingness.

From the Bridge

Did you ask when?
I lacked the curiosity
to approach the man,

leaning down as he was,
and breathing heavily
into the wind...

There is no sense in anything.

The Perplexity of Boxes

An empty box
is only as much as
you make of it.

To live in a box
is not satisfactory.

To die in a box
is better,

more tidy,
provided its dimensions
are to your liking.

To be dead in a box
could be to
lie more happily.

Coda

Strike up, Ye Minstrels

This is scarcely the moment to bore us
by laying out old facts in his case again.

We are all so abundantly comfortable now,
here at the sea's edge foregathered.

Waiters arrive, minute by minute,
with spiritous liquors so pleasing to the lips, the stomach.

Women are preparing their various embellishments, I note,
on the further side of the curtaining.

And we are all in such a heightened mood of good cheer
that no one would wish to darken the proceedings

even by so much as a smidgen
by raising the matter of that man again –

why and how they bundled him away into the ground
on such a day at such an hour.

This is not the time or the place
              for such doom-dark delvings.

Strike up then, ye minstrels, strike up,
              without needless delayings!

THE END

www.ingramcontent.com/pod-product-compliance
Lightning Source LLC
Chambersburg PA
CBHW021144080526
44588CB00008B/209